That Shakespeherian Rag

That Shakespeherian
Rag

essays on a critical process

Terence Hawkes

METHUEN

London and New York

First published in 1986 by
Methuen & Co. Ltd
11 New Fetter Lane, London EC4P 4EE

Published in the USA by
Methuen & Co.
in association with Methuen, Inc.
29 West 35th Street, New York, NY 10001

Typeset by Scarborough Typesetting Services
and printed in Great Britain by
Richard Clay (The Chaucer Press) Ltd
Bungay, Suffolk

British Library Cataloguing in Publication Data
Hawkes, Terence
That Shakespeherian rag: essays on a critical
process.
1. Shakespeare, William – Criticism and
interpretation
I. Title
822.3'3   PR2976

ISBN 0 416 38530 3
0 416 38540 0 Pbk

Library of Congress Cataloging in Publication Data
Hawkes, Terence
That Shakespeherian rag.

Includes index.
1. Shakespeare, William, 1564–1616 – Criticism and
interpretation – addresses, essays, lectures.
2. Literature and society – addresses, essays, lectures.
I. Title.
PR2976.H385   1986   822.3'3   85-29713

ISBN 0 416 38530 3
0 416 38540 0 (pbk.)

Still to Ann

It is remarkable how hard we find it to believe something that we do not see the truth of for ourselves. When, for instance, I hear the expression of admiration for Shakespeare by distinguished men in the course of several centuries, I can never rid myself of the suspicion that praising him has been the conventional thing to do; though I have to tell myself that this is not how it is. It takes the authority of a *Milton* really to convince me. I take it for granted that he was incorruptible. – But I don't of course mean by this that I don't believe an enormous amount of praise to have been, and still to be, lavished on Shakespeare without understanding and for the wrong reasons by a thousand professors of literature.

Ludwig Wittgenstein, 1946

Contents

Preface

Earlier versions of parts of this material have appeared in different contexts. Nevertheless, they share the same field of interest as those written with this collection in mind to an extent that made it seem worthwhile including them in the present volume.

Not that the result can claim a status higher than that of the slightest series of sketches, made in the shadow of a number of immense, beckoning models, each with its own array of perplexities and problems. I am not sure that I have avoided any of them. However, I can report that an early impulse to call the book *Eminent Shakespearians* was quietly and efficiently throttled, and that I am grateful to its assassins. Stephen Potter's *The Muse in Chains* (1937), with its compelling account of 'Variorum' Furness, impenetrably both deaf and American, remains seductive, though I have mounted a resistance to it in the name of high seriousness. Meanwhile, Alfred Harbage's underrated *Conceptions of Shakespeare* (1966) continues to set standards of scope and urbanity which have proved impossible to match.

What remains is haunted by the ghost of a larger design. To its importunate cry of 'Remember me!' I can only respond that this, perhaps, represents a start.

Portions of this material have been published in different forms elsewhere. A version of Chapter 3 appears in John Drakakis (ed.), *Alternative Shakespeares* (London, Methuen, 1985). Chapter 4 incorporates material that first appeared in *Essays and Studies 1977* (The English Association) and in Sidney Homan (ed.), *Shakespeare's More Than Words Can Witness* (Lewisburg, Pa., Bucknell University Press, 1980). Parts of Chapter 5 have appeared in *Encounter* (April 1983) and a fuller version in Patricia Parker and Geoffrey Hartman (eds), *Shakespeare and the Question of Theory* (London, Methuen, 1985). Some paragraphs in Chapter 6 draw on material contributed to *The Times Higher Educational Supplement*. I am grateful to the editors and publishers concerned for permission, where relevant, to reprint, refashion or refurbish.

Some of this material has also formed the basis of lectures delivered at a number of institutions: Tulane University, New Orleans, in the United States; the universities of Melbourne, Adelaide, MacQuarie and La Trobe in Australia; the University of Tübingen in West Germany; the universities of Tokyo and Nagoya in Japan; the National University of Singapore; at a conference in Sicily organized by Taormina Arte; at a meeting of the Associazione Italiana di Anglistica in Siena and at a conference 'Shakespeare Today' organized by the Faculty of Magistero of the University of Florence; at the Royal Shakespeare Theatre Summer School in Stratford-upon-Avon; at the British Council Summer School in Cambridge; and at conferences at the universities of Birmingham and Leicester. I am grateful to my hosts and to my audiences for their observations and their forbearance.

I am also grateful to a number of individuals who have taken time and trouble to make helpful comments on my ideas and, with shaming frequency, to suggest better ones. They include John Drakakis, Malcolm Evans, Edmund L. Epstein, Derek Longhurst, Keir Elam, Edwin Thumboo, Stanley Wells, Howard Felperin, David Greensmith. The kindness and keen percipience of the late Bernard Beckerman demands special mention and deserves a better memorial.

Participants in the Cardiff Critical Theory Seminar will know how much I rely on their special brand of convivial acuity, and I am particularly grateful to Catherine Belsey, Andrew Belsey, Christopher Norris, Robert Stradling, John Hartley, Brian Doyle, Chris Weedon and David Goldwater for their often extensive help. Needless to say, all errors are my own.

My students at University College, Cardiff, have continued to be tolerant and receptive beyond the call of duty.

Finally, my greatest debt of gratitude remains: to my wife.

T.H.
University College, Cardiff

1

Playhouse–Workhouse

Tempest and chips

I am eating fish and chips in Stratford-upon-Avon. To be precise, I am doing so while leaning on a lock-gate at the point where the Stratford canal flows into the river Avon. Slightly to my left is the Royal Shakespeare Theatre where I have just attended a performance of *The Tempest*. Slightly to my right is a fish-and-chip shop.

A major concern of this essay lies in the encounter of Nature and Culture. Stratford, both a natural and cultural centre of England, seems to offer a particularly fruitful location in this respect. Here a river (Nature) joins a canal (Culture) in a setting where one kind of Englishness (the Royal Shakespeare Theatre) confronts another (a fish-and-chip shop) in the sale of quintessentially English goods. Here, certainly, one Stratford appears to engage with its opposite. My capacity to ingest both fails to allay a sense of broad and potent distinctions.

One of them, suitably transmuted, lies close to the heart of *The Tempest*, that late play traditionally supposed to have been written here in Stratford. We can begin to discern it in the opposition of Prospero to Caliban. Some of the detailed symbolic freight of that confrontation will be further unpacked at subsequent points in this book, but we can start by sketching some of its general implications.

Master of Arts

Most critics would recognize in *The Tempest* the lineaments of the 'pastoral drama' described by Frank Kermode.[1] Focusing on the opposition of Nature and Culture, pitting their representatives, Caliban and Prospero, firmly against each other, this seems to be the play's organizing principle. And in the context of contemporary Elizabethan and Jacobean concerns with the reinforcement and development of the settlements in the North American New World, the conflict takes on, as Kermode and others have argued, a 'colonial' dimension.[2]

Elizabethan expansion to the West readily prompted metaphors of the 'planting' and 'cultivation' of new growths, whether of tobacco and other crops, or of new forms of social life itself. The 'plantations' of Ulster and of Virginia and the stratagems and concepts these provoked for dealing with an indigenous population generate a discourse which propels a good deal of the imaginative writing of the time and occasionally pushes it to the limits of sense:

> *Guiana*, whose rich feet are mines of golde,
> Whose forehead knockes against the roofe of Starres,
> Stands on her tip-toes at faire *England* looking,
> Kissing her hand, bowing her mightie breast,
> And euery signe of all submission making,
> To be her sister, and the daughter both
> Of our most sacred Maide: whose barrennesse
> Is the true fruite of vertue, that may get,
> Beare and bring foorth anew in all perfection,
> What heretofore sauage corruption held
> In barbarous *Chaos*; and in this affaire
> Become her father, mother, and her heire.[3]

The colliding figures of fruitful kinship reeling through such verses nevertheless suggest a complex context in which the trope of Prospero as Planter, with the aboriginal Caliban as unnourishable growth or Slave seems reasonably straightforward and unexceptionable.

However, the matter has dimensions which perhaps derive from a rather more deeply rooted experience than the relatively immediate one of the colonial enterprise. Of course, the texts relating to that enterprise inhabit the same discursive field as *The Tempest*, deploy the same presuppositions, and accept the same map of the conceptual terrain. The story of the wreck and subsequent miraculous preservation of Sir Thomas Gates, Sir George Summers and the company of the *Sea Adventure* in the Bermudas in 1609 was widely known. William Strachey's *A True Reportory of the Wrack and Redemption of Sir Thomas Gates* may in any case have been seen in manuscript form by Shakespeare, and further details could easily be found in Silvester Jourdain's *A Discovery of the Barmudas, Otherwise called the Ile of Divels* (1610).

But the complex relationship between Prospero and Caliban hardly springs from these 'sources'.[4] Its basis lies in the operations of a discourse which precedes and generates all of them: one whose systematic disposition of categories developed nearer home, rooted in and geared to long-embedded political notions familiar enough to all British citizens, including those who had never travelled further west than Stratford itself. If the colonizers brought a ready-made framework of ideas with them and if, like most travellers, they never ventured beyond its horizons – indeed, imposed these on whatever novelties confronted them – then it seems reasonable to suggest that the roots of the Prospero–Caliban relationship extend beyond that of Planter to Slave to find their true nourishment in the ancient home-grown European relationships of master and servant, landlord and tenant.

Thus the tropical 'paradise' described by Gonzalo (II. i. 138ff.) turns, for definition, on legal notions with whose precepts and consequences most of the audience would be familiar, since they touched their daily lives: 'contract, succession,/Bourn, bound of land, tilth'. And those issues probed at the centre of the play involve moral concepts long invested in the mundane business of the diurnal round. As a number of critics have noticed, the task of carrying logs, an appropriate and familiar emblem for the brute manual work, the 'wooden slavery' as Ferdinand punningly calls it, that was a standard feature of quotidian British life, clearly functions as a symbolic means of contrasting Ferdinand with Caliban. Thus it lends the 'captive log-bearing Prince' motif recognized by Kermode the additional dimension of more immediate social commentary. Ferdinand acknowledges the moral – not to say social – profit which accrues to his labour, and in consequence bears his burden willingly:

> I must remove
> Some thousands of these logs, and pile them up,
> Upon a sore injunction: my sweet mistress
> Weeps when she sees me work, and says, such baseness

3

Had never like executor. I forget:
But these sweet thoughts do even refresh my labours,
Most busilest when I do it.

(III. i. 9–15)

Although Miranda readily offers to share his task (III. i. 23–4),
Ferdinand manages to reconcile himself to it in the name of love:

> for your sake
> Am I this patient log-man.

(III. i. 66–7)

Caliban, by contrast, bears logs only unwillingly. The play
clearly nominates his work as straightforward slavery from the
beginning, and our initial encounter with his disembodied voice
takes place in that confirming context:

Prospero: . . . What, ho! slave! Caliban!
          Thou earth, thou! speak.
Caliban within: There's wood enough within.

(I. ii. 315–16)

Repeatedly urged to 'Fetch us in fuel; and be quick' (I. ii. 368),
Caliban bears his 'burthen of wood' (II. ii. s.d.) with an appropriately ill grace, reinforced by curses against his masters and his
wretched fate.

In Ferdinand's case, then, work seems to be a burden which,
nobly borne, offers plentiful compensation. His attitude thus
accords well with a range of moral doctrines that colonization
claimed to substantiate, and confirms an overall position
succinctly expressed in the disgust with which Strachey cites the
reports of some of the colonists:

> An incredible example of their idlenesse, is the report of Sir
> Thomas Gates, who affirmeth, that after his first comming
> thither, he hath seene some of them eat their fish raw, rather
> then they would goe a stones cast to fetch wood and dresse it.
> (cit. Kermode, p. 140)

But the moral drawn by the reports resolves into an apothegm
which doubtless would have sprung no less readily to the lips of
many a contemporary Elizabethan employer on his native soil:
'*Dei laboribus omnia vendunt*, God sels us all things for our labour'
(ibid.). Caliban's complete refusal of this principle finds an

4

appropriately revolutionary mode of expression when he turns
the log-bearing exercise neatly against Prospero, advising his
fellow conspirators on the efficacy of a 'log' to 'batter his skull'
(III. ii. 87–8).

Clearly a major contradiction stares at us here, threatening to
dislocate the bars of the discourse which cage it in the play. It
centres on the familiar paradox of work. From one point of view,
work traditionally represents a punishment inflicted on human
beings as a penalty for Adam's sin. And the play seems to endorse
this, to the extent that Ferdinand's patience with respect to his
work will be rewarded by the ultimate removal of its burden.
Indeed, he is a clear candidate, on the island, for membership of
that perfect world outlined by Gonzalo, in which work would be
proscribed altogether:

> All things in common Nature should produce
> Without sweat or endeavour
>
> (II. i. 155–6)

However, Antonio's comment that the result of such idleness
would be a society of 'whores and knaves' (l. 162) rests on a
wholly opposed view: that work is good: it restrains carnal
appetite and channels human energy to useful, moral and socially
supportive ends. A related paradox obviously operates in respect
of work's opposite. The absence of work, conceived as leisure or
play, can only rank as good. But the same condition can also
result from indolence, and that makes it the breeding ground of
turpitude. If Gonzalo's vision of perfection attempts to straddle
the contradiction –

>   no kind of traffic
> Would I admit . . .
> No occupation; all men idle, all;
> And women too, but innocent and pure
>
> (II. i. 144–51)

– its unavoidable chasms yawn in the punctuating, deflating
commentary supplied by Sebastian and Antonio, and they gape
wider and wider in the opposition drawn between the attitude to
work of Ferdinand and Caliban.

The play clearly uses that opposition as the focus through
which it presents the relationship of each to Prospero. And this

relationship involves power. In effect, Prospero deploys manual work as the negotiable instrument by whose means his power can be ratified and reinforced. Ferdinand's acceptance of work's moral, restraining function and the commitment to harmonious social order which that signifies is both rewarded and symbolized by his winning of Miranda's hand. But Caliban's rejection of work and thus of the subservience to which the relationship with Prospero condemns him smoulders throughout as a disturbing threat until it irrupts into actuality at a crucial moment in the play.

In effect, his master-murdering projects draw him into the referential field of a specific Elizabethan and Jacobean bugbear, the 'masterless man' who haunted the margins of that society and (supposedly) the suburbs of its cities. Ungoverned, unrestrained, challenging from the periphery the central ligature on which social order rested, such a figure offered fertile ground for the seeds of moral panic. The very label 'masterless', clearly signalling a refusal of a power-relationship based on servitude and work, served to define and intensify the role of masters and even to establish a sense of corporate identity among them.[5]

The play carefully sets Caliban in, or places him against a landscape whose pastoral mode conflicts with and offers to comment on his own unmitigated and potentially unmastered savagery. The graceful dancing of idealized Reapers, the 'sunburn'd sicklemen' with their 'rye-straw hats' and their 'country footing' conjured up by the goddesses Juno, Ceres and Iris, takes place in a kind of idealized Warwickshire landscape from which the overt signs of manual work have been decorously drained:

> *thy rich leas*
> *Of wheat, rye, barley, vetches, oats and pease;*
> *Thy turfy mountains, where live nibbling sheep,*
> *And flat meads thatch'd with stover, them to keep;*
> *Thy banks with pioned and twilled brims,*
> *Which spongy April at thy hest betrims*
>
> (IV. i. 60–5)

Nobody seems to toil in this agrarian paradise of bursting plenitude:

> *Earth's increase, foison plenty,*
> *Barns and garners never empty;*

Vines with clust'ring bunches growing;
Plants with goodly burthen bowing

(IV. i. 110–13)

And yet, clearly, this pastoral pageant (produced and directed by
Prospero) serves to support an established and work-dominated
social order, to which it might be said to bring spectacular reinforcement. As Louis Adrian Montrose points out, the pastoral
mode in the Elizabethan and Jacobean period had a central political function in its 'symbolic mediation of social relationships',
relationships which were 'intrinsically relationships of power'.[6]
It is appropriate, then, that Prospero the master, the power-
broker, is also here the play-maker, the pastoral-monger. If
playing, and the use of drama and spectacle, performed a sustain-
ing ideological role in this society, it clearly also sustained the
currency of work in which the society dealt. By means of such
'playing', for instance involving the spectacular trappings of the
legal system and its recourse to ostentatious, publicly displayed
punishment, masters established a work-enforcing magistracy
over their servants. In this sense, play meant work: or rather,
play enabled work to mean – to signify the extent and purpose of
its economic, political and social office.

When thoughts of the revolution planned by 'the beast Caliban'
begin to impinge upon Prospero's pastoral play-world, its 'majestic vision', as Ferdinand calls it, disintegrates, the revels end,
their fabric dissolves, and nymphs, reapers and sicklemen vanish
'heavily'. As if in sympathy with that disruption we also hear
what the stage direction terms 'a strange, hollow and confused
noise'. To twentieth-century ears, it might for all the world be a
shop steward's whistle or a police siren.

Pursued by a beare

It is a noise which draws us irresistibly to the Midlands. Indeed,
in so far as *The Tempest* has been thought to have been written in
Shakespeare's retirement in Stratford, with the Bard himself cast
as the retiring magus, those 'turfy mountains where live nibbling
sheep' have been assigned a local habitation, with their hint of a
characteristically English pastoral scene, fondly drawn from the
memory and experience of the Warwickshire playwright.

7

And yet if we follow that process through, forgetting for the moment the New World exotica, something rather disturbing begins to happen to the sheep. They undergo a bizarre transformation, even a reversal, of their traditional pastoral role.

Enclosure was in the air. This reorganization of methods of working the land helped reshape the contours of the world in which Shakespeare grew up and lived, and on a national scale constituted part of a drive towards what we might now call cost-effectiveness. Essentially, it involved the amalgamation of the ancient medieval strips of land, farmed by individual tenants, into much larger units farmed more profitably by fewer people. To 'enclose' land was to consolidate its resources in the name of efficiency. Frequently the aim of the landowner was to produce by this method larger units of pasture-land for the grazing of sheep. And with a smaller number of shepherds tending the flock, the profits from the sale of wool would be correspondingly greater.[7] Enclosure also buttressed the master–servant relationship because it helped to flush out the 'multiplicity of beggars' and other masterless men known to congregate on unenclosed 'common' land. In 1610 James I encouraged the House of Commons to adopt a programme of enclosure that would rid such land of the numerous cottages that acted as 'nurseries and receptacles of thieves, rogues and beggars'. Enclosure could thus be regarded, Christopher Hill reports, 'as a national duty, a kindness in disguise to the idle poor'.[8]

Unfortunately, enclosure also required the dispossession of a large number of small tenant farmers who accordingly became, as we might say, redundant. Effectively, then, the investment in sheep turned out to be a major factor in the growth of a particular phenomenon: one that we have had to recognize as a continuing feature of the modern world heralded by the enclosure movement. Christopher Hill points out that a major consequence of that movement was that it forced its victims into 'sole dependence on wage labour'.[9] Wage labour involves a concept of work as a quantifiable activity, engaging specific services for a specific period and for a specific purpose. For some the justification of enclosure lay in its power to coerce its victims, however unwilling, into an acceptance of that model. As Adam Moore writes in 1653, enclosure 'will give the poor an interest in toiling, whom terror never yet could enure to travail'.[10] And Hill indicates that by 1663 enclosure was in some quarters pronounced successful on just those grounds: 'people were added to the manufacturing population who previously did not increase the store of the nation but wasted it'.[11]

If we call that notion of work *employment*, we can see it as an outgrowth of a number of sixteenth- and seventeenth-century developments in which enclosure was prominent, and we can also recognize it as an innovation to be set against an older concept of work involving an entire way of life which does not distinguish 'toil' as a quantifiable entity from a broad range of other activities. And in its shadow we can see the outline of a concomitant innovation with whose later complexities we are wholly familiar: *unemployment*. To create the one is to create the other.

Of course, this immediately makes problematical a set of inherited polarities nominating work as good, idleness as bad, since it transfers the principle of enforcement from the one to the other. The prospect of an enforced, involuntary and unwilling idleness clearly eats away at and contradicts the moral imperatives invested in Prospero's and Ferdinand's notion of work.

In short, and despite the prevailing pastoral mode, we might begin to wonder just what those nibbling sheep in *The Tempest* were effectively nibbling at. For to Sir Thomas More even in the previous century they had conjured up a vision precisely the opposite of pastoral in mode: a nightmarish spectacle in which, where once men devoured sheep, now sheep devoured men.

If it seems fanciful to propose that *The Tempest* shared the conceptual horizons or the discursive 'field' of the enclosure movement, it may be helpful to recall one aspect of its author's contemporary context. Like Prospero, he had recently become a landlord.

On 24 July 1605 Shakespeare invested £440 in a half-interest in the tithes deriving from the hamlets of Old Stratford, Bishopton and Welcombe. In September 1614 the landowners Arthur Mainwaring and William Replingham proposed the enclosure of an area of land in close proximity to Stratford, specifically at Welcombe. Shakespeare and other tithe-owners, including Thomas Greene the town clerk of Stratford, were offered assurances that any loss of income to them resulting from the enclosure would be recompensed by the landowners. In return, they were asked not

9

to oppose the move, and possibly to give it their support. For its part, the Stratford corporation vehemently opposed the enclosure, expressing considerable concern about the hardship this would inflict on the tenants and their dependants. They required their town clerk, Greene, to represent these views both to the landowners and to Shakespeare, in an effort to dissuade the former and to persuade the latter to throw his influence (and perhaps artistic fame) behind them. Greene visited Shakespeare and his son-in-law, Dr John Hall, in London, and records their efforts to calm him and the corporation by assurances that the landowners 'meane in Aprill to servey the Land & then to gyve satisfaccion & not before & he & Mr Hall say they think there will be nothyng done at all'. Later Greene reports an unsuccessful attempt to confront the landowners at Shakespeare's house in Stratford, and speaks of letters written to them and to Shakespeare which describe the 'Inconvenyences which wold grow by the Inclosure'.

The affair escalated when William Combe, another wealthy local landowner, joined in the movement to enclose, and arranged for the digging of a ditch on his land as an initial stage in marking the enclosure. Corporation officials tried to prevent this, and violence ensued. Combe persisted and something of a local riot followed. The ghost of Caliban confronted the spirit of Prospero as women and children from Stratford and Bishopton marched out and filled in the ditch as a demonstration of their views. There was further violence, and feelings ran high. Shakespeare seems to have made no move to support the corporation and his involvement in the affair reaches an appropriate climax in a brief but deeply mysterious text. This is an entry in Thomas Greene's diary which records: 'Sept. W Shakspeares tellyng J Greene that J was not able to [word deleted] beare the encloseinge of Welcombe.'

Plurality invests all texts of course, but none more so than this. Its very subject guarantees it a talismanic, even votive status in our culture which offers to propel the words beyond the mere page. They seem to present, after all, a record of oral utterance, of actual speech on the Bard's part which, at this date, might almost lay claim to the aura of last words, significant beyond the context of their saying.

Certainly the diary itself projects the entry into a peculiar time-less prominence, since it was clearly made outside the usual temporal sequence characteristic of diaries. The manuscript shows it to be a later insertion, a 'retrospective memorandum' as its editor calls it, of an event whose significance is thereby greatly increased.[12] 'J Greene' probably refers to John Greene, the brother of the diarist. But the second 'J' who was 'not able to beare the encloseinge of Welcombe' presents an unresolvable ambiguity, a complex *aporia* of broad implication. For the peculiarities of Thomas Greene's handwriting permit the sign here lamely recorded as 'J' to function as 'J' or 'I' or even 'he'. Thus an entire spectrum of potential meaning offers itself since the reference could be to any of the three persons involved. So the entry can indicate that 'J' (i.e. John Greene) was unable to bear the enclosing of Welcombe, or that 'I' (i.e. Thomas Greene) was unable to bear it or, more poignantly, that 'he' (i.e. Shakespeare) was in that situation.

A further complexity resides in the word 'beare'. A contemporary range of potential meaning for the word extends from our modern sense of 'endure', through 'justify' and 'support', to the rather more problematical, even opposite sense of 'promote' or 'carry through' or even 'bear the cost'. The fact that Greene evidently deleted what looks like the beginning of a different word before 'beare' indicates that it may have given him pause too.

Scholars will of course habitually select specific readings of texts and defend them, to the point of rejecting or denying the fruitfulness which this sort of undecidability brings. My argument nevertheless suggests that the ambiguities complicating the entry in Greene's diary serve to fissure that text well beyond the level of its surface, and help to establish that, like all texts, it has no claim to be autotelic, prescribing its own boundaries, determining the limits of its own meaning. Its own historical 'moment' cannot confine it (indeed, by the standards of the diary genre its subsequent insertion marks it as 'out of' sequential time), nor is its range of signification determined by its ostensible concern with a particular matter of real estate. The issue of Elizabethan land enclosure generated questions which potentially obtruded into the discourse of morality, politics and economics both at that time and subsequently. The text of Greene's diary concerning the enclosure of Welcombe also enters and operates within those fields: it links up with a 'network' of discourses running in and

11

out of a variety of other texts as part of a process of *intertextuality* which enables all texts to signify not discretely, by themselves, but structurally, by means of their relationship to each other.[13]

This principle suggests that the magisterial figure of the landlord who confidently parades and enforces established notions of work and idleness in *The Tempest* must be set against – and be made far more complex by – the rather more querulous figure (whoever 'J' is) glimpsed at Shakespeare's elbow in Greene's diary. And the 'brutishness' which colours Caliban's militancy in that play must be perceived through – and also be made more complex by – the sense the same text gives of the compulsions propelling the wretched women and children of Stratford and Bishopton, as they marched on Welcombe.

For the burden of unemployment, our latter-day experience should tell us, is as hard to bear as the burden of work. The range of meaning open to the word 'beare' in Shakespeare's day extends disconcertingly from Prospero's confident promotion of Caliban's dispossession on the one hand (he can 'support', 'justify', 'carry it through') to the evident waning of confidence and resolution experienced by some of its proponents unable to cope with the opposition of the citizens of Stratford to the enclosure of Welcombe. It would be misleading and even falsely reassuring to try to resolve the ambiguities of any of the texts which come to us from the years between 1610 and 1614 when, living in Stratford, writing *The Tempest*, Shakespeare was also involved in a developing relationship with his fellow citizens for which the available discourses offered a specific and contradictory set of positions and oppositions. But we can try to recognize what those ambiguities and contradictions involved and the discursive process of which they formed part. As with Prospero, the situation yields a play-maker who is also a power-broker in a setting in which playing reinforces a master–servant relationship based on the social currency of a particular concept of work. Play thus means work, or enables work to mean.

That the creator of Prospero and Caliban should find this contradiction unbearable is not beyond belief. Ideology works to efface contradiction, and the effect of that is to make any sustained contemplation of its implications both alienating and insupportable. But in any case the extent and degree of Shakespeare's purely personal involvement is not in question here. It is the textual and contextual ambiguities and contradictions in and around *The Tempest* that speak of it as a battleground in a contest whose contours prove instructive when viewed from our own arena. And if Shakespeare or his contemporaries found the contradictions of enclosure difficult to bear, we might reflect on our own situation in respect of a cognate economic climate and its fruit.

Cal

If the 'beare' pursues us, the sheep do not. One of the ironies of Stratford's development lies in the fact that the growth of the fame and influence of its playwright son eventually brought that particular wheel full circle. E. K. Chambers records the sixteenth- and seventeenth-century use of the common pasture at the centre of the town for the purpose of grazing sheep.[14] The area was known as Bank Croft. The modern visitor, stepping on to what is now called Bancroft Gardens, encounters in place of the sheep the majestic pile of the Royal Shakespeare Theatre. It is attended by quite a different flock. First people devoured sheep, then sheep devoured people and finally, in Stratford it appears, Shakespeare has devoured everything.

Whether the women and children who stormed the fields at Welcombe would have approved of the development is another matter. Would they even, we can wonder, recognize the landscape they lived in and fought over, once it had been Shakespearianized in our century's characteristic mode?

About a mile out of the town at Longbridge the road bifurcates, the way to the left going through Barford and Wellesbourne, where there is a turn to Charlecote, that to the right going up Sherborne Hill, past Coplow Hill, leaving Snitterfield on the right, and then descending through park-like lands, past the mansion of Welcombe, backed by low hills, till it skirts the level meadows through which the Avon flows, and so enters the town of Stratford-upon-Avon.

The little town of Stratford-upon-Avon, built on the river banks, and surrounded on all sides by meadows and green fields, like a coral island set in an emerald sea, is one of the pleasantest places of the earth.

(*Picturesque Warwickshire*, 1906, pp. 68–9)

That can be called enclosure with a vengeance. The ruthless amalgamation, consolidation and reduction of a complex topography by means of a teleological bulldozer forces it to become the ground of a massive industry.

The ideological mode of the Shakespeare industry can be said to be centripetal, integrating. In the middle, geographically and metaphorically, of a potentially tempestuous and certainly volatile industrialized society, not thirty miles from concrete conurbations the size and nature of Birmingham and Coventry, the guidebook casts us upon an enchanted coral island, set in an emerald sea. Organic in its social structure – the clientele who attend the 'bijou theatre beside the Avon' balanced by the crowds who throng the annual fair where 'a very different scene is enacted' (p. 72) – the island is full of noises, resounding to the

> cries of the stall-keepers and screams of laughter from youths and girls bent on enjoyment. . . . In every street oxen and pigs are being roasted whole, and the air is filled with the savour of dainties dear to rustic appetites.
>
> (ibid., p. 73)

And as the pageant develops, a Prospero-like voice unfolds the full binding and knitting-together purpose of the revels over which, magus-like, it appears to preside.

> The pious enthusiasm which of old led men and women to visit the shrines of saints and martyrs in these days has another outlet. . . . The cottage in Henley Street, now guarded with care as great as that once extended to the sacred flame in the temple of Vesta, the chaste goddess of the hearth, is the great meeting-place for all familiar with the English tongue, exactly as in Roman days Vesta's temple was the sanctuary which united the citizens into one large family. The simile may be carried even further. In those ancient times the hearth in every home was regarded as a symbol of the chaste goddess; we feel sure that no English home is worthy of the name where a copy of Shakespeare's Works cannot be found. To us these mighty poems represent the embodiment of our national spirit. They show us the path of virtue, and how evil-doing carries with it its Nemesis: they teach us patriotism, the love of our fellow-men, and our love of Nature.
>
> (ibid., pp. 73–4)

Fortunately, the latter-day Calibans whose 'rustic appetites' required them to be instructed in the path of virtue were not without a voice. We even have a kind of access now to a number of those English homes, located in Stratford at precisely this time, where aspects of the national spirit were indeed embodied. One of them, situated not a hundred yards from what was then called the Shakespeare Memorial Theatre, was the home of a formidable woman called Caroline Cook. A twentieth-century Prospero might not unreasonably quail at the thought of teaching her about the Nemesis that dogged her so-called evil doings. And we can be fairly sure that no copy of Shakespeare's works was to be found in her cottage at the corner of Sheep Street and Waterside. She was known, after all, as 'Cal'.

In fact, Cal Cook's home is redolent less of a vague, rusticized 'national spirit' than of something that Ronald Blythe has termed 'the air of a cheerful, dreadful England which would do for you if it could'. Her use of the 'English tongue' in response to those pressures has inevitable recourse to the same linguistic structures as that of Caliban, whose only 'profit' from learning it was that he learned 'how to curse' (I. ii. 366). As her protégé George Hewins tells us, the magistrates before whom Cal was hauled on a charge of using 'profane and obscene language' immediately recognized its brutish origins: 'We think it is the most 'orrible, beastly an' brutal language as can be used by one human bein' to another.' Refusing to pay her fine on this occasion, she served a spell in Warwick gaol.[15]

And yet nobody reading Hewins's penetrative story in *The Dillen* can be repelled by these descendants of the women and children who marched out to halt the Welcombe enclosures of three hundred years earlier. And no one can fail to respond to their situation and what it represents. Shakespeare, Combe and their fellow enclosers may have failed to achieve their ends in the past, but success of a much more substantial nature awaited them in the future. By the early twentieth century, embodied in his Memorial Theatre, Shakespeare was a major Stratford landlord. In ideological terms he was a major British one: fount of the national culture, spring of the national spirit, *fons et origo* of patriotism, love of fellow men, love of nature, and most other precepts of a world view which systematically made Prosperos of the few and Calibans of the many.

In Stratford itself the irony naturally had a fine edge. For the bulk of its citizens, as *The Dillen* makes clear, the dominating features of life seemed to have nothing at all to do with the Bard, and centred on the difficulties of getting adequate food, shelter and money. The central features of life for these citizens were the police and the workhouse. Fear of the latter went deeper than anything represented by the former.

In due course, we learn how Cal's family acquired a new landlord. His name, intriguingly, seemed also to rise from within a literary discourse. Indeed, it had a fine Dickensian ring: Salt Brassington. And appropriately enough, in addition to being a landlord, he also fancied himself as an author. The words quoted above which describe Stratford and the rustic lineaments of our national spirit were in fact written by Salt Brassington and are taken from his book *Picturesque Warwickshire*, one of a number of works in which he introduced the splendours of his native heath to a wider world. It is worth remembering that the mellifluous, expansive phrases which list the beauties of the borough and the duties which they involve –

> unless some measures are taken to preserve the ancient character of the buildings, Stratford will lose the quaint old-world appearance so dear to artists and antiquaries, so highly appreciated by American and Colonial visitors. . . . To me it seems to be a sacred duty to preserve the ancient characteristics of Stratford[16]

– are those of a landlord. And it is no less salutary to reflect that the man who speaks, Prospero-like, in favour of the redemptive nature of work and in praise of the 'picturesque' features of the Stratford almshouses –

> Here twelve poor men and twelve poor women spend the last years of their lives, if not in luxury, at least in comfort. Long may such institutions flourish and increase, that those who have worked hard in their younger days may entertain the lag end of their lives with quiet hours.[17]

– brought eviction and the dreaded workhouse closer to his own tenants by a ruthless programme of raising the rent. As the final irony it is only necessary to add that Salt Brassington was an official of the Shakespeare Memorial Theatre and acted as its Librarian.

Once again, power seems to lie with the makers of plays: those who control the dramatic symbolization of social relationships also control a relationship based on work. George Hewins's account leaves us in no doubt that the issue is of that order, with its stress on work's structured, penalizing absence:

> That winter and the next was terrible hard, terrible. The men had no work, no dole. The women couldn't go mangeling, they couldn't pull the mangels up, they was froze in the ground. They got chilblains on their hands; those as went washing or charring like Widow Bayliss came home crying where the soda had got in the cracks. Old folks died of the cold. The young uns like us with families growing had to scratch their heads to know how they was going to live.

But Shakespeare's librarian (the image of Prospero intensifies) remains unmoved:

> To start with, our rent was three shillings and threepence. We'd got a new landlord – Salt Brassington, he was Librarian at the Theatre – and he put it up from half-a-crown a week to *three-and-three*! If you didn't pay the rent you was chucked out. Folks as couldn't pay – if they was old or there was illness in the family – they ended up in the workhouse. Old Bill Hinton went in – Brassington upped his rent from three bob to five-and-six! – and the Rowe family off the street. They couldn't pay. It was a sad sight to see them go. The landlord sold their stuff – put the bailiffs in to get the money for the rent. Cal had two mats off them.
>
> (*The Dillen*, pp. 71–2)

If we set Hewins's vivid, rebarbative account of life in Stratford against the measured prose of Salt Brassington, and thus set a 'native' guide to the borough against an official 'planter's' version, the social map it draws presents an alternative set of dimensions. They can be discerned right from the beginning, in Hewins's account of the hearing held to establish who his real father might be (he was born illegitimate). The Mayor of Stratford, Charles Edward Flower no less, presided as magistrate, and gave judgement in the case with a dispatch not unconnected with another birth in which neither paternity nor legitimacy were in dispute:

> He was busy laying plans for the opening of the new Theatre, just a few days hence, on Shakespeare's birthday. He'd given the land for it, and a lot o' money asides, and it was going to be a really posh occasion. All the toffs would be there – nobility! Stratford was going to get *tone*. . . . 'The defendant can pay three bob a week for the babby' he said, 'and all the costs!'.
>
> (ibid., p. 7)

Whether the mayor realized it or not, the two 'babbies' over whose birth fate had given him jurisdiction were to prove emblems of a new polarity: one in which Flower's role as a magistrate merged fittingly with his role as promoter of drama. For where the world of the magistracy would focus on the Playhouse, that of their servants would focus on the Workhouse. And in truth much of the actual 'tone' of Stratford seemed to derive from that structural opposition.

We follow the fate of the Rowe family:

> I was doing a job at the workhouse, slating the roof. It was a bitter cold morning when we started, frost was in the air and I reckoned it could be my last chance o' work for a while. The door opens and the slummocky roadster woman they'd got for a nurse brings the babbies out, one by one. They'd messed themselves. She peels their clothes back and swills them under the pump like so many winter savoys. November and ice-cold water! They screamed! Those screams echoed round that square yard, hit the high brick walls o' the workhouse – and the roof, where I was.
>
> The older kiddies starts to congregate. Who should I see but Hilda Rowe and Violet. They'd had their hair chopped off, weared long holland pinnas with big red letters: STRATFORD-ON-AVON WORKHOUSE. They did some sort o' drill, then they was marched in a straight line to the National School across the road. The babbies' screams and those red letters haunted me all day. If I weren't hearing the one I was seeing the other. When I got home I told the missus but she said: 'It's to *distinguish* em.'
>
> (ibid., p. 72)

The story of the hapless Rowes, evicted because of their inability to pay Salt Brassington's rent, hints at a symbiotic relationship between Playhouse and Workhouse. And any attempt to 'distinguish' the one institution, as the big red letters try to do, fails to suppress the hint that perhaps it represents the price paid for the other institution, with its eye firmly on 'distinction' of another sort. That the playhouse, and those rustic English cottages in which copies of Shakespeare's mighty poems embody the national spirit, could only be sustained by harsh rent increases and the looming workhouse suggests a contradiction that the best might find difficult to bear. Once again, play seems to mean work. The ironies locked into that situation and their precise location in Salt Brassington's dual involvement should not be lost on us. They were certainly not lost on George Hewins. They were part of the rent he paid:

> Well, we was behind with it, but not badly.
> 'I'll make it up,' I said, 'Didn't you tell er? When I gets work.'
> She plonked herself down on the chair. She was near her time. 'Er says e wants to see you now.' she said. 'I told er to bugger off. I knows it bain't er fault – but it made me feel better!'
> We looked at each other and laughed, cos there seemed nothing else to do.
> 'I'll go an see Cal.'
> 'No!' said the missus. She and Cal didn't get on. 'There must be summat else. I could ask Kate.' Kate Tappin was her elder sister. They was well off, but they'd got kiddies of their own.
> 'I can see Tommy forkin out for our rent!'
> I had an idea, so I said: 'If that's what e wants – I'll go and see ole Brassington!' I went to the Theatre and there was Salt Brassington sat at a desk with a pen in his hand. He didn't look up.
> 'Yes?'
> I held my tongue – and my temper. It was an effort, I can tell you. 'There ain't no work at present – you can see for yourself – it's snowed up.' Still he didn't meet my eye.
> 'I'm a bricklayer by trade – but I can whitewash, and do odd jobs, plumbin an gas, set my hand to *any*thin,' (*to pay the rent*, I thought) 'and I'm good wi a spade. I knows I didn't pay last week . . .'
> 'No,' he said.
> '. . . But I could make it up. I could work for you! I'd be cheap! Handy for you!'

19

That did it! Salt Brassington looked at me: 'Fit man, are you?' He looked long and hard at me, took in every detail. 'Alright!' he said. 'You can clean my windows – you knows where I live, up Rowley Crescent – paint my house for me inside and out. I want some frames for my plants and a gate makin so's to cut off a corner and when spring comes you can mow my lawn –'

He smiled: 'I'm writin a book,' he said, 'on the cottages of England.'

(ibid., pp. 76–7)

The tale of two landlords

No Prospero ever made the point more clearly to his log-bearing Caliban. And while it may be inherently unfair to compare any man with the Bard, it seems not unreasonable to set these two Stratford landlords side by side for a moment. When we do so, what becomes immediately, astonishingly clear is that William Shakespeare and William Salt Brassington share a common role. They are tellers of tales. More, the tales that they tell in Stratford, Shakespeare's *The Tempest*, Brassington's book *Picturesque Warwickshire* and other works, are not at all dissimilar, for a common discourse inhabits and governs both. Both speak of nature and of culture. Both examine closely knit cultural groups. Both can be read as indicating a clear preference for a particular social relationship in that group, a magistracy under whose terms the roles of master and servant, landlord and tenant are willingly undertaken and dutifully sustained as in a play. Both depict a sympathetic landscape on a magical island as an appropriate context for this play. Both see the play, and its container the play-house, as the magisterial bearer of culture to an otherwise unredeemed nature. Both advocate a deferential relationship as the basis of that culture, one cemented by a common commitment to manual work as the outward and manifest sign of subservience. Prospero's relation to Caliban –

> We cannot miss him: he does make our fire,
> Fetch in our wood, and serves in offices
> That profit us.

(I. ii. 313–15)

20

– makes clear a discursive and so political principle in which, across the centuries, George Hewins's children find themselves swiftly schooled:

> They was too famished to learn much. After school, to make a few pence, they got wood from the timber yard and went round Stratford selling sticks, to anybody who wanted firewood.
>
> (*The Dillen*, p. 120)

It follows that to challenge that principle is to find oneself excluded from the social realm constructed by the 'play', from the 'house' of the society in which it is enacted, and even from the almshouse and the 'quiet hours' it promises. It is, as the Rowe family, as Hewins's mother, and as Cal herself finally discovered, to enter a house of quite a different kind.

Of course, the actualities of material existence have a complexity that no fiction can match. The women and children who tried to fill in the encloser's ditch at Welcombe can hardly be embodied in a Caliban. Nor can the grateful accepting souls who inhabit the almshouses of which Salt Brassington so fondly writes reflect the ribald sardonic tenantry to be found in Cal Cook and her brood at the corner of Waterside and Sheep Street. Neither could form part of any tale of picturesque Warwickshire.

But that is why such tales exist. Human beings cannot bear very much reality. The attraction of tales lies in their capacity to present a reality that human beings *can* bear: to paper over the cracks, resolve, explain and make coherent the contradictions. It is what tales are for.

And so the argument is not that Shakespeare was in any way simply dramatizing his personal experience: the fact that the events at Welcombe occurred a good five years after the writing of *The Tempest* tends to dispose of that. Instead, the causal sequence might be emphatically reversed, particularly if we think of 'personal' experience as necessarily embedded in and moulded and transmitted by the shaping forces of literary or cultural discourse. That is what enables it to be experienced. It is not that the enclosure at Welcombe underlies *The Tempest*. It is that the discursive categories and stratagems which *The Tempest* inherited and developed perhaps underlie the enclosure at Welcombe. Thus the question to be asked is not the rather naive one posed by Edward Bond's play *Bingo*: how could the man who

21

wrote the great tragedies behave as he did in the face of suffering humanity? The more probing enquiry asks how could he not?

In the case of Salt Brassington, similar conclusions are appropriate. It is the discourse of 'country cottages' which enables, justifies even, the actions of the rack-rent landlord, as the interchange with Hewins quoted above makes clear. The work Hewins is charged to do as a way of paying off his obligations supports the writing of the book on country cottages, and is responsive to that book's demands: Brassington's performance as landlord reproduces the presuppositions of the guidebook discourse and is shaped by its categories and its teleological imperatives.

If the spectacle is one in which both Stratford landlords effectively operate within and by means of a pre-established framework, then a final irony inheres in our own shorthand account of the mode of that discourse as 'Shakespearian'. For while this places Brassington in a well-established tradition of latter-day 'users' of the Bard, it also suggests that the first user of that discourse, its first prisoner, was Shakespeare himself.

That the Prospero–Caliban relationship should offer itself across the years as a model for subsequent social and political alignments is not surprising: it confirms the potency of the figure. Trevor R. Griffiths reports that the first 'overtly republican' Caliban appears in the production of William and Robert Brough's *The Enchanted Isle* in 1848. Uttering anti-slavery slogans, this monster entered to the strains of the *Marseillaise* 'with a Cap of Liberty on his head' and 'a red flag in one hand'. His ultimate surrender to Prospero acknowledges through its absurdities the serious political issues at stake in that year:

> Governor, we surrender at discretion,
> And to your government send in adhesion.
> We own that this a just and fair defeat is
> So take these chains off and let's sign some treaties.

The American civil war generated a Caliban in a *Punch* cartoon of 1863 who in the guise of 'Sambo' offered a 'nigger translation' of *The Tempest* tailored to fit that conflict, and throughout the later nineteenth century numbers of theatrical productions featured a Darwinian 'missing link' Caliban who was also the 'undeveloped' native in need of control by the civilizing colonialist intellect.[18]

22

It will be clear that I take Brassington, seen in the round both as landlord and as custodian of the archives of the Shakespeare Memorial Theatre, as a symbol for a larger enterprise: one which involves our society's recuperation and sentimentalization of a moment in its own history of four hundred or so years ago. That moment is sensed as crucial, and it will be the purpose of the subsequent essays in this book to examine some of the ways in which the twentieth century puts it to use. In so far as both in himself and in his actions Brassington embodied polarities which our century has seemed unquestioningly to accept – on the one hand a notion of redemptive Culture, on the other a notion of brutish Nature, Playhouse and Workhouse – he remains a remarkable and richly significant figure, fit to be juxtaposed with his fellow citizen under the aegis of the giant modern industry which both ultimately served. The ironies generated by that industry lie all about us and perhaps we hardly need the nudging of which Hewins proves himself slyly capable. Yet the spectacle of his progress, by now severely wounded in the Great War, without work of course and reduced to begging from door to door in Stratford, has its telling moments:

> 'Wait there' said one bloke. I thought I was in luck. He gave me a book: *The Complete Works of William Shakespeare. A book!* Somebody had writ inside: 'It is hoped that this will always keep you in mind of the true greatness and glory of the cause for which you have fought and suffered.'
>
> (*The Dillen*, p. 159)

To step back finally into generalities, it would be misleading to present what I have obviously conceived of as an archetypal encounter between Prospero and Caliban as if it were a straightforward confrontation of polarities and to leave it at that. Culture and Nature are not the simple opposites we tend to presuppose in our covert preference for one over the other, and convincing arguments exist to persuade us that what we call 'nature' is really just a special case, if not a deliberate invention, of what we term 'culture': that Prospero actively constructs Caliban as part of a complex self-establishing process perhaps recorded in his admission, 'this thing of darkness I acknowledge mine'.[19]

Certainly, leaning on the lock-gate at the point where the Stratford canal (preserved these days, weed-strewn and rustic, by the

National Trust) becomes the river Avon (surely one of the major 'cultural' constructs of an English-speaking world), a confusing confluence becomes self-evident. It should be added that while to my left there certainly stands the relatively new cultural edifice of the Royal Shakespeare Theatre (the building so dear to Salt Brassington having succumbed to natural forces, a fire, in 1926) the establishment that confronts it to my right, the fish-and-chip shop, has little enough claim to be a spontaneous popular out-growth of the town's English inheritance. Several ironies invest it. First, it stands exactly on the site of Cal Cook's cottage at the corner of Waterside and Sheep Street. Second, it now rejoices in the name of *Dillen's Fishery*, after Hewins's successful book (published by the Oxford University Press) and thus exhibits dis-cursive dimensions no less literary or prestigious than those of the establishment to which I have opposed it. The whirligig of Time brings in his revenges. The opposition, in which one citizen of Stratford (William Shakespeare) confronts another (George Hewins), is as complex as those other oppositions in which Play-house confronted Workhouse in the early years of the century, or enclosers confronted women and children three hundred years before that. And it is certainly no less complex than the oppo-sition in which Prospero confronted Caliban or cultured Eliza-bethan planters confronted brutish Indian natives in the Virginia colonies in North America.

Indeed, the highest level of complexity was perhaps reached when George Hewins and his wife found themselves, at the urging of Salt Brassington, working respectively as 'super' (i.e. extra) and dresser at the Shakespeare Memorial Theatre. It was the result of further 'difficulties' connected with the rent, of course, and the work exacted finally did establish the sort of symbiotic link between Playhouse and Workhouse that has been proposed above. We can note that Frank Benson, the resident company's leading actor, found it amusing to speculate that some of the Stratford aboriginals might even be descendants of Shake-speare. He had an interest in savagery after all, being famous for his portrayal of Caliban. Constance Benson tells us that he spent 'many hours watching monkeys and baboons in the zoo, in order to get the movements in keeping with his "make-up"'. He also carried a real fish in his mouth, and an eye-witness of his performances between 1900 and 1924 records that 'It added to the realism of his missing-link Caliban that he could clamber nimbly up a tree and hang head downwards from a branch, chattering with rage at Prospero.'[20] Critical insights of this order ensured that the representative of Culture in Stratford was in no doubt of the place in the scheme of things occupied by the natives: they could only be instances of unredeemed Nature: ' "Course," 'e says, "they'll be *bastards*, Harry – bound to be!" We all laughed.' (*The Dillen*, p. 124).

It was almost the last laugh. Because if Benson's initiative resulted in the paradox of a bastard Hewins/Caliban who finally knew *Hamlet* legitimately 'by heart, without a book' and could recite chunks of it (ibid., p. 123), that was only the prelude to an ultimate irony when, in 1983, the Royal Shakespeare Company presented a dramatized version of *The Dillen*, not in the theatre but in a series of 'actual' locations in the town of Stratford itself, using present-day townspeople in the performance.[21]

But by then, the long four-hundred-year process which saw Stratford completely colonized by its playwright Prospero was virtually over. The ditches dug to define the theatre's province had extended far beyond Bancroft Gardens to undermine the very phonetics of local speech. And as, at the corner of Waterside and Bridge Street, not a hundred yards from Cal Cook's cottage, the old *Anchor Inn* finally dwindled into the new *Encore Inn*, the full stratagems of a conclusive play-maker/power-broker amalgamation revealed themselves, intent on subsuming all Stratford houses, not to say English-speaking culture at large, in its magisterial, Shakespearianizing theatricality. The complications and scale of that sort of enclosure generate a sizeable speculative burden. If we find it difficult to bear, we might reflect that at least, once, we were in distinguished company.

Notes

1 *The Tempest*, Arden edn (London, 1954), xxiv.
2 See Trevor R. Griffiths, ' "This Island's Mine": Caliban and Colonialism', *The Yearbook of English Studies*, 13 (1983), 159–80.
3 George Chapman, 'De Guiana, Carmen Epicum' (1596) in *The Poems of George Chapman*, ed. Phyllis Brooks Bartlett (New York, 1941), 353–4.
4 See the argument of Francis Barker and Peter Hulme, ' "Nymphs and Reapers heavily vanish": the discursive con-texts of *The Tempest*' in

John Drakakis (ed.), *Alternative Shakespeares* (London, 1985), 191–205.

5 See Christopher Hill, 'Masterless Men' in *The World Turned Upside Down*, Penguin edn (Harmondsworth, 1975), 39–56; A. L. Beier, *Masterless Men: the vagrancy problem in England 1560–1640* (London, 1985); and Paul Brown, '"This thing of darkness I acknowledge mine": *The Tempest* and the discourse of colonialism' in Jonathan Dollimore and Alan Sinfield (eds), *Political Shakespeare* (Manchester, 1985), 48–71.

6 Louis Adrian Montrose, '"Eliza, queene of Shepheardes" and the Pastoral of Power', *English Literary Renaissance*, 10 (1980), 153–82.

7 See Peter J. Bowden, *The Wool Trade in Tudor and Stuart England* (London, 1962).

8 Hill, op. cit., 51.

9 ibid., 53.

10 ibid., 52.

11 ibid., 51.

12 C. M. Ingleby (ed.), *Shakespeare and the Enclosure of Common Fields at Welcombe: being a fragment of the Private Diary of Thomas Greene, Town Clerk of Stratford upon Avon 1614–1617* (Birmingham, 1885), v–vi.

13 On the concepts of intertextuality and discourse and how these may be fruitfully applied to *The Tempest*, see Barker and Hulme, op. cit.

14 E. K. Chambers, *William Shakespeare, a study of facts and problems* (Oxford, 1930), 1, 9.

15 Angela Hewins (ed.), *The Dillen: Memories of a man of Stratford-upon-Avon* (Oxford, 1982), 4. For Ronald Blythe's comment, see p. v.

16 W. Salt Brassington, *Notes on the Old Houses in Stratford-upon-Avon* (privately published: the Walsall Press, 1899), i.

17 W. Salt Brassington, *Picturesque Warwickshire* (London, Edinburgh and Dublin, Valentine and Sons, 1906), 80.

18 See Trevor R. Griffiths, op. cit.

19 See Paul Brown, op. cit., and also Stephen Greenblatt, 'Invisible bullets: Renaissance authority and its subversion' in the same volume.

20 Trevor R. Griffiths, op. cit., 166–8.

21 In 1985, Angela Hewins edited a volume of memoirs by Mary, George Hewins's daughter, entitled *Mary, After the Queen* (Oxford, 1985). As part of its summer season in that year, the Royal Shakespeare Company presented a dramatization of the book, to run in tandem with a revival of *The Dillen*.

2

A Sea Shell

Harsh words

It was quite a scandal. The authorities objected strongly to his teaching. In their view it was dominated by a rigid foreign 'system' imported from Europe; obscure, mystifying and replete with 'fuliginous jargon'. Its alien metaphysics exercised a fatal influence over the minds of undergraduates, destroying or at least undermining their British commitment to straightforward empirical observation, and certainly endangering their chances in the university examinations, where the examiners were known for their hostility to this kind of abstract vaporizing. Worse, the ideas involved had clear, and possibly radical, social and political implications.

The Master felt his world begin to crumble. Formerly an enthusiast, even something of a 'revolutionary' (he had been called a 'heretic' years before), he now had little tolerance for this new, foreign, politicized professionalism which was invading his subject. These youngsters took a specialized and systematic stance far removed from the rather genteel mode in which he was accustomed to operate. They were not content to teach, to aim at producing fully rounded gentlemen. They favoured rigorous training in the subject and, horror of horrors, postgraduate research, even the establishment of readerships in the field, committed to the prosecution of new work within it.

The ringleader, a former friend and current colleague, was invulnerable. But his subordinates were not. Accordingly, they were edged out, firmly and decisively: in this particular case 'expelled' in the words of one commentator, 'martyred' in the words of another. Angry letters passed, tempers were lost, friendships broken. Eventually the young man obtained another appointment in a new and soon vigorously expanding field. It led, not without acrimonious comment in the press, to a chair in Scotland. He became famous.

No doubt this has a familiar ring. However, the full ironies of the story emerge when we reflect that these events took place just over one hundred years ago, in Oxford. The subject involved was philosophy, the Master was Benjamin Jowett, the college Balliol. And most interesting of all, the name of the 'martyred' young man whose career, apparently blighted, was then so decisively revived in a new field by everything that happened, was A. C. Bradley.

Spreading the word

The family name of Bradley echoes across the Victorian period in a vast sonorous intellectual peal. Andrew Cecil Bradley was born in 1851. His father, Charles Bradley, was an Evangelical minister, well known as a member of the so-called Clapham sect. His half-brother, George Granville Bradley, was head of Marlborough School, then Master of University College, Oxford, and later Dean of Westminster. His sister, Harriet Bradley, married George Grove, man of parts, editor for a number of years of the prestigious *Macmillan's Magazine*, whose major achievement was perhaps the monumental *Grove's Dictionary of Music*. His older brother was F. H. Bradley, the idealist philosopher whose work became the subject of T. S. Eliot's doctoral thesis, and ostensibly the reason for that poet's momentous crossing of the Atlantic just before the outbreak of the First World War. Between them, the Bradley family can be said to have had a considerable influence on the fledging academic subject of 'English' which was invented in their lifetime.

Bradley's doubts concerning his father's Evangelical faith, with its belief in the 'unmediated interpretation of the Bible' and the 'literal truth of scripture' are well attested.[1] There is even talk of a 'spiritual crisis' in the sickly youth, resolved only when in 1869 he entered Balliol College, Oxford, where he encountered the teaching of the man who was the mainstay of the group of British idealist philosophers whose work was having such an intense impact: T. H. Green. Green, Bradley is reported to have said, 'saved' his soul – a feat something of whose dimensions forms the substance of Mrs Humphry Ward's novel about Green (whom she named Grey), *Robert Elsmere*.[2] So saved was he that in 1874 he became a fellow of Balliol, where he taught Philosophy.

According to G. K. Hunter, Bradley's debt to Green is 'quite specific'. It consists, in religious terms, of substituting a Broad Church theology for the more direct claims of Evangelicalism, and as a bulwark against the conservative reaction of High Church theology. In political terms, Green represented that peculiar English confection made from Hegel and an uneasy conscience, Liberalism. Significantly, Bradley was made a Fellow of Balliol on the same day as Asquith. To quote Melvin Richter:

> Between 1880 and 1914 few, if any, other philosophers exerted a greater influence upon British thought and public policy than did T. H. Green. . . . Green converted Philosophical Idealism, which in Germany had so often served as a rationale of conservatism, into something close to a practical programme for the Left Wing of the Liberal Party.
>
> (*The Politics of Conscience: T. H. Green and his Age*, p. 13)

Green's efforts, as a Broad Churchman, to drop the traditional dogmatic and historically based theology of Christianity in favour of a restatement based on idealist metaphysics could be seen as a direct Liberal challenge to authority, but his embracing and 'liberalizing' of Hegel came to seem an uncritical Germanophilia which gradually effected his own estrangement from Jowett.[3] Jowett's native empiricism clashed directly with Green's idealism, particularly as this grew into the basis for a more 'professionalized' approach to philosophy.

Green's battles to establish philosophy as 'an autonomous professional discipline' (as opposed to a branch of the study of Classics) in fact follows an impetus of Jowett's whose reforms sought to enable philosophy to serve the Broad Church movement.[4] Rejecting the old doctrines of authority, as Richter says, the new subject sought to teach the history and method of thought, to encourage independent thinking, to teach its students how to think, not what. Green, in Richter's words, 'was certainly the first Fellow of his College, and possibly the first in the University, to conceive of himself as a professional philosopher' (ibid., p. 140). Jowett's disapproval was directed towards what he saw as that philosophy's unwarranted systematization and its separation as a discrete subject from other branches of learning. He stopped Green, and Green's pupils, from conducting tutorials, and his deliberately engineered expulsion of Bradley must be seen as part and parcel of what Green called Jowett's desire 'entirely to expel philosophy from Balliol'.[5]

The details of Bradley's exit remain clouded, but Richter speaks darkly of his 'martyrdom', and a sort of apocalyptic air hangs over the episode. Perhaps we can sense in it the dawn of modern academic specialization and the beginning of a new abrasive mode of secular education. Certainly the pupil of the first 'professional philosopher' left Oxford to become one of the first professional teachers of a new subject: English.

He began at the University of Liverpool. Having applied for a chair in Philosophy and Political Economy, he found himself in fact appointed in 1882 as the first holder of a new chair in Modern Literature and History. After an unsuccessful application for the Merton chair of English at Oxford in 1885, Bradley left Liverpool in 1889 to become Professor of English at Glasgow University. It was this appointment that aroused the notice of the journal *Truth* run by the journalist and MP Henry Labouchère. *Truth*'s comment carries more than a hint of the competitive pressures that professionalization brings with it:

> The appointment by Lord Lothian of Mr A. C. Bradley to the Chair of English Literature at Glasgow has given deep offence in Scotland, and, most assuredly, it seems to be an arrant job, for there were several gentlemen whose claims were far superior to those of Mr Bradley, which, indeed, rest on a very shadowy foundation, for his merits are by no means widely known, whereas some of the other candidates had distinctly made their mark in literature.   (*Truth*, 1 August 1889, p. 195)

In 1900, at the age of 49, Bradley took what we would now call early retirement and moved to live in London. And then, in the next year, came the event which affected not only his career, but the intellectual life of the English-speaking world and beyond to a considerable degree. He was made Professor of Poetry at Oxford. **It was the return, in a sense, of the repressed.**

To say that this post generated some of the lectures which we now know as the substance of Bradley's book *Shakespearean Tragedy* (1904) is to minimize its importance. In fact, it guaranteed the publication of all of them – together with a number on more disparate subjects, published as *Oxford Lectures on Poetry* in 1909 – and in so doing established one of the most influential texts of our century: one which by now ranks as almost synonymous with the study of 'English' and which, despite earnest efforts to unseat it, remains a key, and vastly formative work. Bradley's *Shakespearean Tragedy* is one of those books whose influence extends far beyond the confines of its ostensible subject, permeating the attitudes to morality, psychology and politics of hundreds and thousands of English-speaking people, regardless of whether or not they have ever set eyes on the text. It has the authority – not unquestioned of course – of the divine scriptures (ironically the sort of authority which Green taught their author to question) and, along with works such as *Scouting for Boys* and *Hymns Ancient and Modern*, exercises the kind of invisible or subliminal influence on our view of the world that proves deeply and lastingly persuasive. Still in print (a new edition appeared in 1985), Bradley's *Shakespearean Tragedy* almost functions, through a system of universal education which has established the study of Shakespeare as its linchpin, as part of the air we breathe.

The former rebel philosopher, returning in triumph, and translated to another dimension, thus exacted a peculiar but not unfitting revenge in Oxford. Through him, it might be said, Philosophy found itself subverted by Literature. Together with Classics it sank, in terms of broad social influence, virtually without trace. English became the huge and continuing success of the academic world, carrying all before it as the requirement for social and professional advancement; for instance, in the Civil Service. A famous comic verse of the 1920s celebrates the inextricable links between the most important names in exactly that mode:

> I dreamt last night that Shakespeare's ghost
> Sat for a Civil Service post;
> The English paper for the year
> Had several questions on *King Lear*
> Which Shakespeare answered very badly
> **Because he hadn't read his Bradley.**[6]

Words on the page

'His' Bradley: the possessive conveys a paradoxical universalizing dimension, stressing the necessity and inevitability of the connection, heightening it, even, and certainly undermining it by means of the comic reversal. The reversal's humour lies in its blithe unconcern for an inherited and implicit notion of the mechanics of 'reading'. It proposes, blandly but mischievously, that we might be able to read history backwards, thus reinforcing a standard 'commonsense' view that in fact we can *only* read it the other way round. Reading, it insists by comically hinting at the reverse, is unfortunately a one-way process.

Bradley would certainly have agreed, and his theory of reading merits a brief examination for the extent to which it can be said to reinforce this notion. In sum, it rests on the idea of language as a transparent and directly expressive medium. Reading takes the reader through the text to make contact with the author's mind whose contents it expresses. It assumes, as a first principle, that the text functions as a reasonably straightforward pathway to that mind, and as a second that there exists a perfect expressive 'fit' between the text and its author's mental processes. The concern of reading is to follow that pathway as closely as possible and so to re-create in the reader's mind the original process of composition, as it occurred in the poet's mind. In a letter to Gilbert Murray (22 September 1901) Bradley makes the point directly: 'Reading or understanding' the poem, he says, will involve the readers in 'making the same process occur in themselves as occurred in the poet's head'.[7] As a result, he argues elsewhere,

> the poem becomes to the reader what it was to the writer. He [the reader] has not merely interpreted the poem, he has recreated it. For the time being his mind has ceased to be his own, and has become the poet's mind.

We should aim, in short, to 'reproduce in ourselves more faintly that which went on in the poet's mind when he wrote'.[8]

Throughout the lectures in *Shakespearean Tragedy*, the final appeal, in the face of abstract, general ideas is always to the concrete reality, and so to the authority of these mysterious processes, presented – whatever else may be claimed – as what actually happens when the critic reads. For instance, speaking

about ideas of Fate in the lecture 'The Substance of Shakespearean Tragedy', Bradley notes that, despite the popularity of
that notion

> I must in candour confess that to me it does not often occur
> while I am reading, or when I have just read, a tragedy of
> Shakespeare. Wordsworth's lines, for example about
>
> > . . . poor humanity's afflicted will
> > Struggling in vain with ruthless destiny
>
> do not represent the impression I receive; much less do images
> which compare man to a puny creature helpless in the claws of
> a bird of prey.
>
> > (*Shakespearean Tragedy*, St Martin's
> > Library edn, London, 1957, p. 22)

And then, as if to reinforce the authority of the personal experience at stake, he adds with the full admonitory force of his
Evangelical background, the stern injunction, 'The reader should
examine himself closely on this matter.'

Whatever the results of such an examination might be, the twin
notions that the words on the page directly and accurately convey
what the author had in mind, and that an honest and open
reading of them if closely examined will yield access to that
mind, clearly operate here. The process involves a text conceived
as perfectly transparent: indeed, its perfection results from its
transparency. When Bradley reads Shakespeare, then, the action
moves entirely one way: the reader checks in, receiving his
boarding pass. Beyond the page there lights up a kind of super-
smooth runway along which the critic's mind energetically
bowls, checking at all times that its responses match the instruc-
tions of the control tower, until it launches gratefully and with
little effort into the stratospheric mind of the master. At this point
the safety belts of close examination may be uncoupled, the cabin
crew smile reassuringly, and the in-flight movie begins.

Lost for words

Let us suppose that the film is called *Hamlet, Prince of Denmark*.
Bradley's famous lectures on this play begin and sustain the close
analytic reading for which he is renowned, and the published

version of them in fact advertises this as the decisive point of departure: a preface to the book refers to the first two theoretical introductory lectures as a desirable prolegomenon, but advises, with British empirical dispatch, that 'readers who may prefer to enter at once on the discussion of the several plays can do so by beginning at page 70'. And that page strikes a dominant note: the analysis presents the issue head on:

> Suppose you were to describe the plot of *Hamlet* to a person quite ignorant of the play, and suppose you were careful to tell your hearer nothing about Hamlet's character, what impression would your sketch make on him? Would he not exclaim: 'What a sensational story! Why, here are some eight violent deaths, not to speak of adultery, a ghost, a mad woman and a fight in a grave! . . .'
>
> (*Shakespearean Tragedy*, p. 70)

However, something quite simple quickly impresses itself upon this querulous exclaiming person: the conclusion, in Bradley's words, that 'the whole story turns upon the peculiar character of the hero'.

In effect, this lecture scrupulously follows the dictum made plain in the introductory lectures, which establishes immediately the essential feature of Bradley's approach: 'The centre of the tragedy . . . may be said with equal truth to lie in action issuing from character, or in character issuing in action' (ibid., p. 7). When he adds 'Shakespeare's main interest lay here', Bradley sets the seal on his whole enterprise. Its focus will be on the reading of character; the inner nature of human beings which determines their deeds and their fate. The dictum that, with Shakespeare, 'character is destiny', may be an exaggeration, he tells us, but only the 'exaggeration of a vital truth'.

Bradley's concern with character has been challenged of course by numbers of critics, specifically L. C. Knights, on the grounds of its reductive nature: it reduces Shakespeare's emblematic, poetic dramas to the level of quasi-realistic portrait galleries of interesting human specimens. It turns the plays into second-rate novels. The same interest has been explained and to some extent justified by G. K. Hunter as a manifestation of the influence on Bradley of Green's Hegelianism. If the tragedies, beyond their surface, give evidence of an 'idealist' dimension, of a general

34

philosophy or meaning (for instance, that the defeat of the tragic protagonist is in the interests of a good greater than himself, as Hunter puts it), then the actions and motivations of the characters in the plays must contain the clues to this meaning (as men's actions do in real life) and can properly be subjected to the closest scrutiny for that purpose. As Hunter argues, 'The world of Shakespearean tragedy is then for A. C. Bradley a world of secular men whose lives yet embody and display the deepest mysteries of our existence.'[9] It is in pursuit of those mysteries that 'character' and the moral choices to which it gives rise are so remorselessly, even obsessionally analysed. The plays become a kind of laboratory in which, under carefully simulated 'real life' conditions, the secrets of existence can be probed.

This is the context, then, in which the analysis of *Hamlet* proceeds. Hamlet's character presents the 'central question' at issue (*Shakespearean Tragedy*, p. 72), and of course the play without that character, *Hamlet* without the Prince, has become a symbol of absurdity. The key to the Prince's character lies in the text, and close reading, close 'attention to the text', repeatedly offers itself as the sole and wholly justifying approach.

Yet remarkably the *Hamlet* lectures proceed to focus a good deal of attention on something that at first sight appears hardly central to the text at all: Hamlet's love for Ophelia. The early reviewers of *Shakespearean Tragedy* certainly remarked upon it. On 28 January 1905, writing in the *Westminster Gazette*, John Churton Collins took Bradley sourly to task on the matter:

> The real points of interest and importance in the drama are not so much as touched on and the particularity with which what is touched on is dealt with is almost invariably in an inverse ratio to its interest and importance. Probably, for example, no intelligent reader of the play has ever had much difficulty in understanding Hamlet's relation to Ophelia – namely, that he was at first passionately in love with her, that then misunderstanding her reserve, and thinking that she was in league with his enemies, he suspected and mistrusted her, but that to the last something of his old love for her remained. This is discussed under nine headings. . . . Every lecture teems with those irritating superfluities, aggravated it may be added by the **unnecessary diffuseness with which they are discussed.**[10]

The essence of Bradley's position lies in the notion that the words on the page transparently express character, and that a vital consistency exists between those elements: 'the text does not bear out the idea that [Hamlet] was one-sidedly reflective and indisposed to action . . .' (p. 86); 'But consider the text. This shrinking, flower-like youth – how could he possibly have done what we *see* Hamlet do?' (p. 80). What Hamlet does is of a piece, consistent: 'Imagine Coleridge doing any of these things' (p. 87) – and the overall principle of consistency extends not only to Hamlet's character, but makes that character consistent finally with the character of Shakespeare himself:

> The truth probably is that [Hamlet's 'characteristic humour'] was the kind of humour most natural to Shakespeare himself, and that here, as in some other traits of the poet's greatest creation, we come into close contact with Shakespeare the man.
> (p. 122)

Even concrete personal experience, shared, it is presumed, by Bradley and his reader, finds itself adduced to substantiate the notion that the text expresses a consistency of character development. Take, he argues, 'the idea that the gift and the habit of meditative and speculative thought tend to produce irresolution in the affairs of life': 'Can you verify it', he thunders, '. . . in the lives of the philosophers, or again in the lives of men whom you have personally known to be addicted to such speculation? I cannot' (p. 92). In real life, as in art, character generates text, text manifests character, and a consistent and perfect 'fit' persists between the two.

Consequently, when Bradley moves to the subject of Hamlet's love for Ophelia, a subject whose importance for him is marked by his decision, he tells us, to reserve for 'separate consideration' this 'important but particularly doubtful point' (p. 103), we confidently expect a close analysis of the text, of the words on the page, in illustration of the argument. In the event, we find quite a different spectacle.

Bradley's problem, like Hamlet's, arises from the question of which of the various conflicting accounts of a particular set of events he is to believe. Certainly Hamlet loved Ophelia. The text offers no difficulties on that point. But as to the course or development of that love in the play, no fewer than three distinct possibilities emerge:

1 What Bradley calls the 'popular' view. This proposes that Hamlet's love for Ophelia never changed, though he was forced to *pretend* that it did, and thus to act 'a part intensely painful to himself' (p. 123). Over her grave, however, the truth 'bursts' from him. Unfortunately, says Bradley, this view fails to take account of certain 'facts and considerations', which he then proceeds to list, to the derision of Churton Collins, under those infamous *nine* headings (pp. 124ff.). They consist of observations such as: 'How is it that in his first soliloquy Hamlet makes no reference whatever to Ophelia?'; 'How is it that in his second soliloquy, on the departure of the Ghost, he again says nothing about her?'; 'Neither is there the faintest allusion to her in any one of the soliloquies of the subsequent Acts. . . . If the popular theory is true, is not this an astonishing fact?'; 'Is there no significance in the further fact (which by itself would present no difficulty) that in speaking to Horatio Hamlet never alludes to Ophelia, and that at his death he says nothing of her?'; 'How is it that neither in the Nunnery scene nor at the play-scene does Shakespeare insert anything to make the truth plain? Four words like Othello's "O hardness to dissemble" would have sufficed.' In short, in all but three of the nine cases cited, what Bradley terms Hamlet's 'astonishing' *silence* on key issues proves a major factor.

These considerations suggest two alternative versions of the course of Hamlet's love:

2 Hamlet's love, though never lost, changed irrevocably as a result of Ophelia's rejection of him, being thenceforth 'mingled with suspicion and resentment' (p. 126).
3 Hamlet's love was not only mingled with suspicion and resentment as a result of *external pressures*, such as Ophelia's rejection of him, but additionally underwent weakening and deadening from *inside himself*, as a result of his characteristic melancholy. This melancholy lay dormant in him from the beginning and woke 'whenever he saw Ophelia' (p. 127). It failed fully to absorb him, or habitually to occupy his mind, but its 'morbid influence' always lay in wait and 'is the cause

of those strange facts, that he never alludes to her in his soliloquies, and that he appears not to realize how the death of her father must affect her'.

Of these three versions of the course of Hamlet's love,

1 That it never changes,
2 That it changes because of external reasons,
3 That it changes because of internal reasons,

Bradley argues that the 'facts' force number three upon us. Once again, he appeals to the coherent 'text' of 'real life': 'psychologically it is quite sound, for a frequent symptom of such melancholy as Hamlet's is a more or less complete paralysis, or even perversion, of the emotion of love' (p. 127).

Yet the plain fact remains that the issue of the course of Hamlet's love for Ophelia depends on elements that are *not* in the text, or on words that Hamlet does *not* say: on his *silence*. This sparks the drama that follows. For given Bradley's commitment to close reading, to 'text', to words on the page, how can he handle silence? And so, having put the case for the importance of the 'internal' operations of Hamlet's melancholy, Bradley recoils in the face of the silence which constitutes its badge: 'yet', he says, 'while feeling no doubt that up to a certain point it is true, I confess I am not satisfied that the explanation of Hamlet's silence regarding Ophelia lies in it' (p. 127). And why is this? Because

> scarcely any spectators or readers of *Hamlet* notice this silence at all; that I never noticed it myself till I began to try to solve the problem of Hamlet's relation to Ophelia; and that even now, when I read the play through without pausing to consider particular questions, it scarcely strikes me.
>
> (p. 128)

This opens a textual drama of Hamlet-like proportions. What is the status of the silence in the text? All texts manifest silence. How do we decide whether or not a silence signifies? Or does all silence signify?

Bradley here runs full tilt into the central issues of textuality. We who, since Freud, since Saussure, since Marx, Barthes, or Derrida, have felt compelled to listen to the sounds silence makes in a text, to respond to what is *not* said as if it were as significant

38

as what is said, can hardly feel superior to Bradley as he wrestles with this matter. We can and should notice that his struggle reveals the nature and limits of the equipment he brings to it. Certainly, his notion of the text as fully expressive of its author's intention proves inadequate:

> it seems at least possible that the explanation of Hamlet's silence may be that Shakespeare, having already a very difficult task to perform in the soliloquies – that of showing the state of mind which caused Hamlet to delay his vengeance – did not choose to make his task more difficult by introducing matter which would not only add to the complexity of the subject but might, from its 'sentimental' interest distract attention from the main point.
>
> (p. 128)

He also suggests that from his theatrical experience, Shakespeare knew that the audience would not notice the silence. But these are counsels of despair. The text has already ceased to be the bearer of coherent, unitary meaning, or the sure base on which a reading can ground itself. Instead, Bradley tells us, 'I am unable to arrive at a conviction as to the meaning of some of [Hamlet's] words and deeds, and I question whether from the mere text of the play a sure interpretation of them can be drawn' (p. 123).

Neither explanation of the issue, he concludes, can be 'more completely convincing to me than the other' and he finds himself 'driven to suspend judgement, and also to suspect that the text admits of no sure interpretation' (p. 128).

Hamlet himself was never more torn, and Bradley's flat conclusion that 'the text admits of no sure interpretation' could effectively stand as a critical epigraph to the play itself. Like the Prince, he finds himself confronted by complex and bewildering contradictions. First, the three versions of Hamlet's love, all derived from the same text, contradict each other in that they claim on the one hand that Hamlet's love never changes, on the other hand that it does. And if change takes place, they suggest that its cause lies on the one hand with external forces and on the other with internal forces. Second, Shakespeare's intentions with regard to Hamlet's silence appear to be contradictory: on the one hand he seems to be offering a complex account of the Prince's motivation by means of his silence; on the other hand the silence, which we fail to notice anyway, seems a way of avoiding complexity.

In short, by noting the text's silences *as part of the text*, Bradley uncovers a vertiginous vista at its centre, a complex self-engendered paradox, in the face of which any readings can only and must always register bafflement. No appeal to 'real life', no urging that the reader should 'examine himself closely', no attempt to make the same process occur in yourself as occurred in the poet's head will discover the unity and coherence, the 'perfection' of fit between text, author's mind and reader's mind that he searches for.

Bradley's disquiet can be imagined. He has encountered a Ghost on the battlements: it brings the alarming news that a text's 'meaning' cannot be limited to the words it uses. The situation wrings from him a further admission, which he subsequently appends to his analysis as he prepares his lecture for the press. It adds an astonishing dimension. If silence speaks in *Hamlet*, does it not do so in every text? Does not this undermine totally the sense of the text as a positively and fully expressive medium? Does not this apply here and now? Reading over his analysis of Hamlet's silence, a shaken Bradley later attaches the disturbing sentence, 'This paragraph states my view imperfectly (p. 128).

With this, the fat drops neatly into the fire. If your account of a text's imperfection states your view 'imperfectly', then the *mise en abîme* has no end: your statement that the text 'admits of no sure interpretation' must *itself* be unsure, and the distinction between the text and your commentary on the text begins to dissolve as an immanent imperfection unites them both.

The moment captures and highlights Bradley's encounter with, and his entrapment in textuality. His statement about the imperfection of his own paragraph briefly illuminates the condition that haunts all the lectures on Shakespearian tragedy: there is – as Derrida puts it – no *hors-texte*: no firm, no perfect ground beyond the text from which to mount an objective survey of its imperfections. It follows that the opposition which Bradley has effectively gestured at throughout his lectures – 'perfect' text (which wholly states the author's view and leads directly to the author's mind) and 'imperfect' text (which doesn't) – cannot begin to hold. There are no 'perfect' texts. Bradley's momentary recognition of wholesale imperfection reveals the truth. Texts 'perfectly' reflect little enough in his limited sense. Their plurality – which Bradley labels 'imperfection' and which, for instance, in the obsessional 'nailing down' process characteristic of the 'notes' at the end of *Shakespearean Tragedy*, he attempts to eradicate – in fact defines them and makes them what they are.

With this granted, the prior opposition, Poet's mind–Reader's mind, with its presupposition of a 'perfect' one-way 'reading' transmission from one polarity through a transparent text to the other, can hardly hold. And the specific 'named' instance of that which has already been mentioned and on which Bradley's enterprise famously depends

Shakespeare–Bradley

thus immediately becomes vulnerable as the names begin to melt into one another. Certainly the opposition which currently concerns us, Shakespeare's text of *Hamlet* as against Bradley's reading of *Hamlet*, must collapse as a result. As it does so, we can surely say that Bradley's reading of *Hamlet*, with its princely indecision, its soliloquizing puzzlement over contradiction, its rapier wit, its melancholic worrying, its weary ultimate consignment of vast interpretative realms (the 'rest') to silence, virtually becomes part of the play. Text and reading intermingle as the one becomes an aspect, or particular instance, of the other.

Far from contradicting Bradley's notion of reading, this extends its implications to the full. The reader, we remember, should not merely interpret the poem, but 'recreate' it. His mind should accordingly cease to be his own and should 'become the poet's mind'. He should make 'the same process' occur in himself as occurred in 'the poet's head', and should aim to repeat and reproduce the mental acts in which the poem exists. The reader should *become* the poet and should relive part of the poet's life.

And the spectacle that confronts us is finally of Bradley's becoming the Bard, of his text turning into Shakespeare's and as an effect of that, of Shakespeare reading and indeed writing Bradley; exactly the picture conjured by the verse about the Civil Service examination. Seen thus, it stretches the rather limited sense of those terms 'reading' and 'writing' which we inherit from the nineteenth century. Shakespeare's texts, processed as they must be by the political and social forces of our society, force

41

a deployment of responses to themselves on the reader (construct-ing in him or her for instance a rage for coherence of 'characteris-ation') which in this case offers to dissolve the Bradley–Shakespeare, reading–writing polarity entirely. To name the one, as we have said, is to name the other. It is almost as if Shakespeare had read, or reached via the text 'his' Bradley, Bradley's mind, and written down a version of what he found there.

Can we not distinguish Bradley from Shakespeare then? Is Shakespeare's text the same as Bradley's account of it? In a complex social sense, by means of that linkage of names which the comic verse insists on, the answer must of course be yes. For thousands of the products of our education system this is the case: a situation which the verse affirms, through its mockery. If Shakespearian tragedy 'reads' Bradley, it is, quite literally, A. C. Bradley who writes *Shakespearean Tragedy*.

To underline the point, we might bring to mind a curious episode in the middle of the lecture on *King Lear*. Bradley is discussing the author's design for the character of the Fool. Suddenly, from the lecturer's mouth, we hear a startling new voice, that of Shakespeare himself:

> I will have a fool in the most tragic of my tragedies. He shall not play a little part. He shall keep from first to last the company in which you most object to see him, the company of a king. Instead of amusing the king's idle hours, he shall stand by him in the very tempest and whirlwind of passion. Before I have done you shall confess, between laughter and tears, that he is of the very essence of life, that you have known him all your days though you never recognised him till now, and that you would as soon go without Hamlet as miss him.   (p. 259)

As the Professor's accents become indistinguishable from those of the Bard (Bradley has asked us to imagine Shakespeare reeling winsomely home one evening from The Mermaid Tavern), a central aspect of his criticism shows its hand. Who, listening to his lecture, could confidently identify or separate the speakers at this point? No 'perfect' answer is possible.

The sound of silence

Perhaps the ultimate critical act occurs when reader merges into writer, lecturer into subject. And in the case of *Hamlet* it is instructive to grasp the degree to which Bradley's analysis finally generates total integration of this sort. The bare biographical information that Bradley himself suffered from 'unrequited love and fits of melancholy'[11] fails to surprise. He aims to go beyond the text, to gain access to the author's mind. But the text, as I hope to have shown, always refuses to yield up that quarry. Instead, rejecting its presupposed separate identity it asserts a paradoxical unity with its interpreter, returning the reader's mind back again, but dressed up as the author's: Bradley, as it were, in doublet and hose.

Silence in any text offers the perfect occasion for this kind of transaction. As we have seen in the case of *Hamlet*, silence gives back nothing. Or, indiscriminately open to interpretation, it gives back anything and everything. If we wanted a metaphor for the process we might consider the sea-shell: held to the ear, it apparently emits the sounds of the sea. But of course the sea-shell does no such thing: it produces no sound. In fact the sound we hear may simply be the sound of the circulation of our own blood. Nevertheless, we impose a meaning on the sea-shell's silence that appears to extend well beyond ourselves. We say that it speaks to us closely, of its own intimate connection with the sea.

As we watch Bradley place Shakespeare's sea-shell text to his ear, we can only guess at the nature of the pressures that have already begun to shape what he is bound to hear. His commitment to a probing of Hamlet's silence accords with a broader contemporary concern, almost ubiquitous at this time, to penetrate silent and unnameable dimensions thought to lie beyond the surfaces of all manner of texts. Conan Doyle's stories of Sherlock Holmes depend on the detective's urgent will to fathom those depths. Oscar Wilde's *The Picture of Dorian Gray* (1891) offers a classic instance of the more sinister deployment of a sense of culpable interiority, and in the specific case of Shakespeare, it is possible to point to Wilde's earlier version of a similar idea in his outrageous peek behind the texts of the Sonnets in *The Portrait of Mr W. H.* (1889) which unveils Willie Hughes to public view. Frank Harris's *The Man Shakespeare* (1909) subsequently proposed a further sensational lifting of the text's façade. The sense of mute and forbidding, not to say forbidden profundities lurking behind bland textual frontages finally and shatteringly surfaced in the trials of Oscar Wilde in 1895, when the text of love

43

itself was forced openly to admit to dark, shameful realms of experience which Victorian Britain had suppressed by a massive silence, commemorated in Lord Alfred Douglas's scandalous reference to the 'love that dare not speak its name'.

An urgent, if not hysterical, public commitment to the naming of that name nevertheless finds expression in the savagery of the sentence passed on Wilde. The Criminal Law Amendment Act under which he was arraigned had reached the statute book only ten years earlier, and the particular clause dealing with his offence had been inserted into it and zealously carried through Parliament by the same Henry Labouchère who had earlier named Bradley in connection with the Glasgow chair. Labouchère's aim, he makes clear, was to force the law and the public to 'take cognizance', as he put it, of activities such as Wilde's. And indeed his lifelong commitment to the boisterous breaking of silence is confirmed by the uncompromising title of his journal, *Truth*, as well as by his general political stance which frequently found a good deal of public support.[12] Conflicting impulses thus seem to confront each other. On the one hand a pressure not to name, to suppress, occlude, obscure: on the other an opposite pressure to nominate, to pierce the veil, to take cognizance.

In 1868, just before entering Oxford, Bradley published a poem in *Macmillan's Magazine*. A conventional, Keatsian piece of juvenilia, it was called, appropriately, 'A Sea Shell':

> Cool lips of shell, sing, Sea-shell, warm and sweet,
>   Of ripples curling on the creamy beach,
>   Of soft waves singing in each other's ear,
> Small wavelets kissing one another's feet,
>   Where flakes of foam make music, a low speech
>   Tenderly sad to hear.
>
> Tell me of half-formed little broken words,
>   Sung by the ripples to the still sea-flowers
>   In silent sleeping tideless deeps of sea;
> For there the flowers have voices like to birds,
>   That sing full-throated in this world of ours   .
>   On each melodious tree.
>
> Not now, not now, sweet shell, some other day
>   Tell me of sighings on the lonely shore,
>   And seas that sob to birds that scream above;

A Sea Shell

Tell me not now of earth grown weak and gray,
  Nor longing for the things that come no more,
      Nor any broken love.

To me thy breathing bears another tone,
  Of fresh cool currents running under sea,
    And happy laughter of the sunny spray:
Ah! hearest thou the words that are thine own,
  Knowest thou the message that they bear to me,
      The things they seem to say?

Ah, Sea-shell, it is this – 'The soft blue deep,
  Which thrills with a heart that knows thee and is kind,
    Sighed for thy sorrow, now it laughs with thee;
Love is a secret which man cannot keep,
  Hide it from heaven and the heedless wind,
      But trust it with the sea!'

Hindsight, or even a less respectable impulse to coherence might urge that the distinction drawn here between the aridity of the land, 'the lonely shore . . . earth grown weak and gray' and the welcoming and comforting depths of the sea hints, albeit damply, at the attraction of those silent, beckoning dimensions to be explored by Bradley's idealism in the years to come, and which subsequently make their formative contribution to his general theory of Shakespearian tragedy. Characteristically, he also insists on the text's transparent connection with actuality, claiming that a reader might make contact through it with its author's mind and with an experience that took place in the real world. He puts this point in his proposal to Macmillan in 1871 that a collection of his verse might be made:

> The poems are arranged in chronological order, for the reason that there is so much change in the subjects and treatment that the book would in this way take an almost biographical form, and I confess one of my reasons for wishing to publish them is the belief that those poems which come near the end of the volume might be of service as well as a pleasure to persons who go through some such experience as is there portrayed.[13]

Macmillan declined the offer. But whatever the nature of the experience at stake, lines such as the last stanza's 'Love is a secret which man cannot keep' seem inextricably involved in the contradictory pressures mentioned above. On the one hand they acknowledge the imperatives of revelation, that love's secrets cannot hope to be hidden; on the other they seem to embrace and even to endorse the comforts of silence and suppression offered by the mysterious sea. The overt complexities at issue for Bradley in Hamlet's unspoken love for Ophelia may or may not be pre-figured here. But certainly the syncopation of half-silence with half-utterance, telling with not-telling, naming with not-naming in which the poem invests projects it firmly towards a cognate nexus of discordant tendencies: a curious discursive arena, its contours made concrete and overt years later in the Wilde trials, where silence paradoxically partners eloquence in a continuing, unfathomable *pas de deux*.

The tensions accompanying an effort to link idealism's cloudy concerns with a politics of practical reality were perhaps already troubling the young Bradley before he entered Oxford and encountered T. H. Green. The 'spiritual crisis' of his youth may have had additional dimensions, but this was certainly an area in which Green's teaching had 'saved' more than one soul. By the time he became Professor of Poetry, Bradley had digested a version of Green's Idealism capable, as we have seen, of fuelling a critical, if not a poetical *modus operandi*.

In fact his lectures mark a moment of significant ideological change. For the years of Bradley's Oxford professorship, after 1901, were also the years which marked the decline of idealism's intellectual dominance of British philosophy. In fact Anthony Quinton goes so far as to nominate 1903, which saw the publi-cation of Bertrand Russell's *Principles of Mathematics* and Moore's *Refutation of Idealism*, as the specific moment of idealism's demise, and thus the end of a hegemony that had begun in 1874. That was the year of Green's critical introduction to his and Grose's edition of Hume's *Treatise of Human Nature*, and of F. H. Bradley's *The Presuppositions of Critical History* and a number of other influential idealist works. The year 1874 also saw A. C. Bradley's initial appointment to a fellowship in Philosophy at Balliol College. Quinton points out that idealism's decline gener-ated the poignant spectacle of ranks of technically unemployable idealists within the philosophical profession. A remarkable num-ber of them dealt with the problem by becoming vice-chancellors.

As Quinton observes, 'The Hegelian mode of thought, with its combination of practical realism and theoretical nebulosity, is a remarkably serviceable instrument for the holders of high administrative positions.'[14] In Bradley's case the fact that the beginning of his career as a professional philosopher coincides with the rise of idealism whilst his tenure of the Oxford Professorship of Poetry coincides with its decline suggests a rather more momentous transfer. In his person, we might say, idealism and liberalism do not decline, so much as migrate with their 'combination of practical realism and theoretical nebulosity' to the new field of English studies where, to this day, in Britain at least, they remain alive and well.

Naming names

The act of taking cognizance, of naming, has always, since Adam, promised a bulwark against chaos. It offers to weld language to the world and the world to language and to use that impacted link as an instrument of control. It was said at the beginning of this essay that the Bradley name rang across Victorian Britain in a great reassuring peal. It seems appropriate at its end to note that Andrew Cecil Bradley's name seems nevertheless to have exhibited a peculiar kind of unsettling potency even before it became widely known. It attracted, as we have seen, the makers of comic verses. It also attracted the constructors of clerihews, that odd and very English investment in the textuality of nomenclature. In common with Curzon –

> My name is George Nathaniel Curzon
> I am a most superior person.
> My face is pink, my hair is sleek,
> I dine at Blenheim once a week.

– and others, Bradley appears in the so-called *Balliol Rhymes* not once, but twice. And in each case he does so with the distinct suggestion that there exist in his person silent and potentially disturbing domains beyond the quotidian:

> I am MR. ANDREW BRADLEY
> When my liver's doing badly
> I take refuge from 'the brute'
> **In the blessed Absolute.**

If that rhyme refers to his then overt professional standing as an idealist philosopher, the other nods decisively in the direction of his competing, albeit covert commitment to literature. Indeed, it pretends scandalously to expose that commitment and mocks its covert nature:

> I'm BR-DL-Y, and I bury deep
> 'A secret that no man can keep'
> If you won't let the Master know it,
> Or F-RB-S, I'll tell you, – I'm a poet.[15]

Part of the humour here lies, of course, in the fact that Bradley's 'secret', given the slightest of homosexual tinges by the quotation of that line from 'A Sea Shell' which chimes with Douglas's 'love that dare not speak its name', emerges comically deflated as a silent 'poetic' dimension looming, unacknowledged and unspeaking, behind his professional role as philosopher. Its effects were also never less than unsettling. J. W. Mackail, who knew him at the time, tries to name this extra dimension specifically, calling Bradley 'an enigma, a veiled poet or a veiled prophet',[16] but only succeeds in confirming that personal *aporia* which the Master of the college's later campaign forced him to confront, and to take a decision about.

Like all texts, clerihews finally give back only the opacity from which they derive. The kind of nomination in which they deal not only forgoes the goal of perfect transparency, it tries deliberately to undermine the project by means of its calculated investment in terse partiality. Thus the clerihew flagrantly abandons any notion of a balanced classification of unchanging permanent reality at which the usual act of naming aims. Systematically, it both names the truth and obscures it, and thus seems well matched, in Bradley's case, to its subject.

Its reward lies in its resultant capacity to achieve a kind of sudden, albeit minor subversion of expectation. Like all successful satire, the clerihew leads us to the edge of a 'named' world, and by undermining names offers to tip us over it. While that impossible feat can never actually be achieved, the attempt hints at that world's boundary, its edge. The clerihew hones that edge sharply.

If, finally, those with Bradley as their subject offer to take cognizance of silent and unnameable dimensions in him, and, in that endeavour, suggest early pointers to the shape of his encounter with the silences of *Hamlet*, the Balliol clerihew on Jowett exacts the cruellest revenge in his name. For the author of Bradley's martyrdom remains himself impaled on a rhyme that presents perfectly the trap of textuality that lay in wait for his generation:

> First come I: my name is Jowett
> There's no knowledge but I know it.

– and it continues in its delicious circularity, to delineate exactly the doom awaiting those who fall into its clutches:

> I am Master of this College
> And what I don't know isn't knowledge.

That last line remains as perfect a statement of silence-effacing self-reflection as any English text has to offer. In it the voice of the sea-shell is heard in the land.

Notes

1 Melvin Richter, *The Politics of Conscience: T. H. Green and his Age* (London, 1964), 25, and G. K. Hunter, 'A. C. Bradley's *Shakespearean Tragedy*', *Essays and Studies*, 21 (London, John Murray for the English Association, 1968), 103.
2 Richter, op. cit., 14. Also J. W. Mackail, 'Andrew Cecil Bradley 1851–1935', *Proceedings of the British Academy*, XXI (1935), 385ff.
3 Richter, op. cit., 27.
4 ibid., 138.
5 ibid., 153.
6 See Katherine Cooke, *A. C. Bradley and His Influence on Twentieth Century Shakespearean Criticism* (Oxford, Clarendon Press, 1972), 191–2 for the text of the verse and a discussion of its provenance.
7 Cit. Cooke, op. cit., 184.
8 Cit. ibid., 50. The quotations are from different sources.
9 Hunter, op. cit., 112.
10 Cit. Cooke, op. cit., 3–4.
11 Francis West, *Gilbert Murray, A Life* (London, 1984), 84.
12 See Hesketh Pearson, *The Life of Oscar Wilde* (London, 1946: Penguin edn, Harmondsworth, 1960), 297. Labouchère's comments make his own position quite clear: 'Wilde and Taylor were tried on a clause in the Criminal Law Amendment Act which I had inserted in order to render it possible for the law to take cognizance of proceedings like theirs. I took the clause *mutatis mutandis* from the French Code. As I

had drafted it the maximum sentence was seven years. The then Home Secretary and Attorney-General, both most experienced men, suggested to me that in such cases convictions are always difficult and that it would be better were the maximum to be two years. Hence the insufficiency of the severest sentence that the law allows.' Hesketh Pearson, *Labby: the life and character of Henry Labouchère* (London, 1936), 242. The sentence was two years' hard labour.

13 Simon Nowell-Smith (ed.), *Letters to Macmillan* (London, 1967), 138–9.
14 Anthony Quinton, *Thoughts and Thinkers* (London, 1982), 186–8. The whole chapter, 'Absolute Idealism', 186–206, repays study.
15 Cit. Cooke, op. cit., 24.
16 Mackail, op. cit., 387.

3

Swisser Swatter: Making a Man of English Letters

Man of Ind

'What have we here? a man or a fish?' It is Trinculo's question, and it is a disturbing one, arising from a confusing encounter. All cultures find themselves impelled to divide the world into the fundamental categories of human and non-human, and when the division between these becomes blurred and uncertain, the effect is undoubtedly troubling.

Trinculo is particularly troubled. His question focuses exactly on that vexing boundary and from the perspective of a European signifying system the lineaments of an exotic, aboriginal or Indian culture are bound to smell fishy. The problem centres precisely on that major cultural question. On which side of the necessary, defining boundary does the creature Caliban fall? Is he a man, or is he something else?

Despite an initial and reassuring location of Caliban as some kind of fishy monster, the possibility that he might at some time and in some place creep worryingly close to the category of 'man' is discussed at some length by Trinculo. It is worrying, of course, because, should Caliban cross that boundary, it would mean that the category of 'man' is not the closed, finished and well-defined entity that sustains and is sustained by a European taxonomy. Even more disturbing, a sly deictic turn of the text suddenly thrusts this possibility down the throat of the play's first, English audience:

> A strange fish! Were I in England now, as once I was, and had but this fish painted, not a holiday fool there but would give a piece of silver: there would this monster make a man; any strange beast there makes a man.

(II. ii. 27ff.)

There is, as all editors note, a slippery quality to the term 'make' here which the text carefully exploits, imposing an economic dimension on an act of cultural taxonomy, and inviting us to see the one through, and thus in terms of, the other. To 'make a man' means to achieve the status of a man, to be ranked in that particular category. But the verb 'make' here also carries the implication of making money for, or making the fortune of, its object. The monster may become ranked as a man or, alternatively, a man can be 'made' (i.e. made rich) by means of the monster. The two sentences 'there would this monster make a man; any strange beast there makes a man' offer in themselves no clues as to which meaning of 'make' is to be preferred in each case. The one is always clearly discernible through the other and the slippage between signifier and signified proves as difficult to control here as it does in the case of the terms 'man' and 'monster'. If any strange beast can make a man, the distinction between these is no simple matter. In the arena of meanings opened up by the text here, classifications which we assume to be settled, objective and definitive appear to fluctuate with the tides of the 'making' market-place: to be determined, at least in England, by the exchange of money.

There are of course a number of reasons why a confusion about the relation of monsters to men should be an aspect of English ideology at the time when *The Tempest* was initially performed. First amongst these must be the impingement on the popular consciousness of the adventures of various groups of settlers on the American continent, particularly their encounter with Indian cultures. Indeed, the making of money by the display of Indians in Elizabethan London was not uncommon and Trinculo's subsequent words refer directly to the practice.[1] The citizens proved regrettably curious in fact: 'when they will not give a doit to relieve a lame beggar, they will lay out ten to see a dead Indian'

52

(II. ii. 32–4). Caliban's status as 'Indian' can be said to be partly confirmed by this, the more so when, moments later, Stephano sees him as part of the armoury of 'tricks' played upon him by the 'devils' of the island: 'What's the matter? Have we devils here? Do you put tricks upon 's with salvages and men of Ind, ha?' (II. ii. 58–9).

In respect of western society, Indians are indeed tricky: they do not make sense. As innumerable Hollywood films inform us, they make trouble. Their presence thus requires an ideological adjustment of a major kind. And as the Elizabethans, that society which initially, for practical purposes, began to make contact with Indian cultures, discovered, the challenge is fundamental. The Indian's meaning undoes our meaning. The Indian's world denies the order and coherence we discover in our world. Only when the disorder and incoherence which Indians represent is subdued to our own and made to serve it, can we make sense/order/money – not of them, so much as out of them.

And of course, whether as inhabitants of the eastern or western peripheries of our civilization (it was a common habit amongst the Elizabethans and Jacobeans to designate the Far West, like the Far East, by the one word 'Ind'),[2] such creatures offered a troubling challenge to a settled European notion of 'manhood'. If Caliban is an Indian, eastern or western, then the question of whether he is a man or not is indeed problematical.

A further dimension of the problem has recently been probed by Peter Hulme, who argues that Caliban's status as a 'man of Ind' in the discourse of Jacobean England falls between, and thus indicates that culture's engagement with, two competing polarities of the exotic, aboriginal challenge to the settled notion of a 'man': the European concept of the 'salvage' or 'wild' man on the one hand, and the newer Caribbean or American concept of the sun-worshipping 'cannibal' on the other.[3] In these terms, Caliban is a figure of considerable ambiguity: an anomaly, a 'compromise formation' of discourses whose figure mediates between two different sets of connotations. Produced in discourse, Caliban proves to be an aspect of a particular struggle carried out in terms of discourse between Europe and America.

To all this, we now have to add one finally confusing feature: Caliban's indeterminate status is irrevocably and ultimately muddled by the fact that, at the height of his interrogation by the egregious representatives of European culture, he emits the major and undeniable signal of genuine manhood: he speaks English. This confuses his discoverers utterly: 'Where the devil should he learn our language?' (II. ii. 67–8) – and it adds the final, undermining touch of ambiguity which then proceeds to permeate the body of the play.

For this short, pivotal scene, right at its centre, starts disconcertingly to unravel an apparently straightforward distinction between monster and man which has seemed thus far to be one of the play's central commitments. Caliban stands, in Frank Kermode's words, as 'the core of the play'.[4] Yet this scene offers us a notion of 'monster' which somehow hovers between contradictory European and American concepts of the outlandish. And it also suggests, in Trinculo's affectionate reference to English habits, the possibility of an alternative to the prevailing European notion of what a 'man' might be. Two possible concepts of 'monster' confront two alternative notions of 'man' here. When the monster then speaks English the inherited opposition between the categories is fundamentally undermined. European notions both of monster and of man, and of the distinctions that may be negotiated between these, confront a challenge – not to say a refusal – in the form of an alternative which is both American and English-speaking. In the monster's own words, the effect is shattering and apparently liberating:

> 'Ban, 'Ban, Cacaliban
> Has a new master: – get a new man.

> (II. ii. 184–5)

But clearly, this array of competing meanings has dimensions which are not inappropriate to a culture which, for profound historical reasons, had by now turned its back on Europe and was looking to the west as a sphere where its own way of life might be re-established, even reborn, in a gigantic exploitative venture.

It is in this sense that *The Tempest* can be said to offer itself as a text whose plurality makes it an arena for the sifting of the immense issue: what makes a man? It is a vitally important question and as a result must surely become the site of the most bitter economic and political competition. Whatever makes a man stands as a major and controlling principle of coherence, both in

terms of the present and the past, in any society. To make a man
is to make sense. And who makes sense, makes history.

Man of letters

Making history, that is making sense of the past in terms of the
exigencies of the present, is a necessary concern of all societies. It
was never more necessary in England than in the late nineteenth
and early twentieth centuries, particularly in that period which
followed the second Reform Bill of 1867. The extension of the
franchise was a disturbing prospect, a massive 'leap in the dark'.
To meet it implied an equally massive effort of incorporation,
inclusion and accommodation; of asserted continuity and of
willed coherence in the name of national cultural identity. The
example of Germany earlier in the century suggested education
as an obvious means by which English Prosperos might domesticate their own Calibans. Thus having new masters, getting new
men, meant, to the prescient, a project whose slogan would urge,
as one minister put it, that 'We must educate our masters'. As a
result, with Forster's Education Act of 1870, Britain embarked on
a system of compulsory primary education which effectively
constituted a drive towards universal literacy. In the next twenty
years the average school attendance rose from one and a quarter
million to four and a half million and the money spent on each
child for the purposes of education was doubled.[5]

It was a revolution, so to speak, by letters. And so it is hardly
surprising that the enshrining, embalming and even the prophylaxis of the national culture took the form so often of monumental
literary undertakings whose purpose was the creation, reinforcement and maintenance of a national English heritage through the
medium of what might be delicately termed English letters. This
is the era of *The New English Dictionary* (later to become the
Oxford English Dictionary), of the ninth edition of the *Encyclo-
paedia Britannica*, of the *Victoria County History* and of that astonishing project the *Dictionary of National Biography*.[6] By June 1894,
the University of Oxford had established its first chair of English
Literature (though it remained unfilled until 1904) and in February 1903 the British Academy was founded.[7]

It was also the era which saw the beginning, in 1878, of a collection of biographical and critical works called *English Men of Letters*.

Published by Macmillan, edited by John, later Lord, Morley, the series found its title only after a certain amount of dithering between revealing alternatives such as *Studies of English Authors*, *Sketches of Great English Authors*, *Lives of English Authors*, *Great English Authors*, *Great Men of Letters*, *Masters of Literature*, and ignobly, *Short Books on English Authors*.[8] However, *English Men of Letters* eventually and significantly triumphed and the series proved an immediate, penetrative and lasting success. In the words of John Gross,

> Right from the start it was accorded semi-official status, and for a couple of generations it remained an unfailing standby for harassed teachers and conscientious students. No comparable series has ever come so close to attaining the rank of a traditional British institution.[9]

Making men of English letters was clearly a powerful way of making British sense and of making world history. Propelled by the immense, formative power of an expanding educational system, the series thus quickly reinforced and became part of the dominant discourse of British ideology.

The fact that, as the volumes succeeded one another, a number of their subjects turned out to be neither English (there was Burns, Burke, Sterne, etc.), nor men (there was Fanny Burney, Maria Edgeworth), nor writers of 'letters' except in an expanded sense of that term (Morley found himself becoming 'more and more averse' to it: 'To call Bunyan or Burns . . . by that title is certainly not good')[10] indicates that anaesthetic power that all discourses possess. They neither disguise nor reveal the truth. The monumentalizing, coherence-generating, sense- and history-making activity of *English Men of Letters* simply *constitutes* the truth: the truth that the true heritage of British culture is written down, and in English, and by men.

Superman

One of the great pinnacles of the enterprise, the jewel in its crown, was bound, of course, to be the volume on Shakespeare, and the Bard was duly constituted an English man of letters in 1907. An appropriate author for this exalted project had not proved easy to find: Matthew Arnold had turned the task down, and in 1877 so had George Eliot, even in the face of a greatly increased fee, thus adding another title to the list of the world's great unwritten books. But at the end of the summer of 1903, man, moment and monument came together. The project was offered to, and accepted by, Walter Alexander Raleigh, then professor of English at the University of Glasgow. He was effusive. 'Two days ago', he writes to Macmillan on 30 August,

> I should have said, with emphasis, that I would never write for a series. But I could not guess that I should be given the opportunity of designing a monument for the poet I love best, in the national cathedral church. The *English Men of Letters* is not as other series are.[11]

In the event, the consequences of having what, in a less formal letter, he termed 'a fling at Bill' were perhaps to justify that last statement. Within a year of beginning work in the national cathedral church, preferment in one of its central parishes had come his way. So fundamental and formative a fling could not be flung in the far North, and Bill's chronicler was appointed to be first holder of the newly established chair in English Literature at the University of Oxford.[12]

At its unveiling, then, in 1907, the monument could hardly have been more solidly based, or centrally placed. Focusing on the figure which, for over a hundred years, had been growing to the stature of cultural superman, obviously designed to become the linchpin of a series which was almost a 'traditional British institution', at a time when the national drive towards universal literacy was creating a mass audience for it, authored by a man whose very name – Walter Raleigh – carried inevitable and appropriate connotations of reassuring contemporaneity, special knowledge, buccaneering glory and a fine literary style, and who was, by then, the first professor of English Literature appointed by the most ideologically central educational institution in the country, the *English Men of Letters Shakespeare* arrived with an aura available to few other volumes before or since. Small wonder that, within four years, the maker of Shakespeare as a man of letters was himself 'made'. Recommended by both Asquith and Balfour in the 1911 Coronation Honours list, he became Sir Walter Raleigh.

'So', this astonishing volume's opening chapter announces with what must be judged a paradoxical air of finality, 'So Shakespeare has come to his own, as an English man of letters.' And in so far as any book is susceptible of a tersely discursive account of its contents, that is what this one single-mindedly sets out to demonstrate. Shakespeare is constructed here precisely in those terms, and to the rigorous exclusion of others that might modify them. Rarely can the manufacturing process of a culture's presuppositions have been so nakedly made visible.

That Shakespeare is English is held to be readily demonstrable, but significantly only in terms of a reduced geographical and racial model which of course sidesteps the thorny, and over the years thornier, question of in what precisely the genuine 'Englishness' of an imperial power (at this time ruling roughly a quarter of the world's population) consists. Raleigh, who had spent two years in India at the beginning of his career, must have known of the cultural complications at stake – the Boer War which raised some of them had continued till 1902. But his book takes a simpler, narrower and more consoling view, endorsing the opinion of 'that excellent antiquary Mrs Stopes' in her conclusion that Shakespeare's pedigree 'can be traced straight back to Guy of Warwick and the good King Alfred' and that this 'noble ancestry' played 'no small part in the making of the poet' (p. 31). That the first sign of this enviable lineage is the Bard's 'unerringly sure touch with the character of his high-born ladies' will prove reassuring to those who persist in finding Lady Macbeth's capacities as wife and mother a cause of some concern.

Shakespeare's engagement with *letters*, i.e. with language in its *written* form, is less easily demonstrable of course, and for a variety of reasons. In a far from wholly literate age, he produced plays: a form of art committed to and involved in language's *oral* form and its visual concomitants. He showed very little interest in preserving his major works in a stable written form, and indeed few absolutely certain examples of his sustained handwriting are known to have survived. However, Raleigh's argument here reaches the heroic pitch appropriate to a wholesale commitment to literacy. Shakespeare cannot be fully appreciated until he is read. Consequently the Folio edition of his plays in 1623, addressed to 'the great variety of readers', marks the beginning of his real fame. From that time onwards (like the race itself

perhaps) it 'steadily advanced to the conquest of the world' (p. 2).
Milton considers him, rightly and simply, as 'the author of a
marvellous book' and 'The readers of Shakespeare took over
from the fickle players the trust and inheritance of his fame.' As a
result 'his continued vogue upon the stage is the smallest part of
his immortality' (p. 2), and his true genius finds itself enshrined
in the fixed certainties which words apparently acquire when
they are written down. It is a matter of demonstrable and inevitable progress to the present: 'While the Restoration theatre
mangled and parodied the tragic masterpieces, a new generation
of readers kept alive the knowledge and heightened the renown
of the written word' (p. 2). And the result is that, in the twentieth
century, just, by chance, as literacy is about to become universal,
so the realization dawns: 'The truth is', Raleigh solemnly assures
us, 'that his best things are not very effective on the stage'
(p. 146). As a result, as English syllabuses begin to be constructed
following the growth of that subject which Raleigh so success-
fully professed, it is Shakespeare's 'book' (p. 25) that becomes so
centrally, so prodigiously – in all its manifold implications – the
ultimate 'set' text. Rather like Prospero's 'book', it offered
power.

Raleigh, it should be said, was always ready to assume the role
of magus in that professional respect. Certainly, more than a
trace of Prospero's megalomania –

> graves at my command
> Have wak'd their sleepers, op'd, and let 'em forth
> By my so potent Art.
>
> (V. i. 48–50)

– inhabits his view of the function of criticism:

the main business of Criticism, after all, is not to legislate, not
to classify, but to raise the dead. Graves, at its command, have
waked their sleepers, oped, and let them forth. It is by the
creative power of this art that the living man is reconstructed
from the litter of blurred and fragmentary paper documents
that he has left to posterity.[13]

Finally, the English writer of Letters must be seen to be a Man.
I have already discussed the notoriously complex issues this
raises for most cultures, not least the one of which Shakespeare

59

himself was (if you'll pardon the expression) a male member. But I'm happy to report that Raleigh's highly potent critical art proves able to cut through these with the dispatch of one to whom maleness is evidently a crucial touchstone of manliness. Shakespeare's standing as an English Man of Letters is vested not in a-sexual social intercourse with its sentimentalized rural decor: the 'dear inanities of ordinary idle conversation' set against the 'lazy ease of the village green' – but in a much more assertive, even aggressive mode of existence where a horny-handed Bard who is 'the greatest of artisans' manifests the starkest kind of maleness, not to say membership, 'when he collects his might and stands dilated, his imagination aflame, the thick-coming thoughts and fancies shaping themselves, under the stress of the central will, into a thing of life' (p. 7). Shakespeare as Phallus of the Golden Age – Phallus in Wonderland – is of course no more peculiar a formulation than many. That he should be thus presented in a context where his potency is diverted and channelled to a national educational drive to universal literacy may seem unduly restrictive, but, again, it is no more peculiar a formulation than many. The pressures and compulsions of ideology are at work here. These are what seek to control the alarming plurality of all texts, and clearly there could be no more effective instrument for such a controlling, prophylactic function in Britain than the aptly named edifice of English letters.

German

Eleven years later a particularly apt instance of this process took place. We can even be quite precise about the date: Thursday, 4 July 1918 – a point in time which has its own resonances, no doubt, but of which, perhaps surprisingly, the Archbishop of York was prepared at the time to say, 'The Fourth of July 1918 will surely be known in after days as one of the great landmarks of history' (*The Times*, 4 July 1918).

The reasons for such a claim are not far to seek. Four years previously, the First World War had plunged Europe into a vast disintegrating crisis, and the resolution of that conflict was obviously a central concern. In April 1917, a major and ultimately decisive event had occurred: the United States of America had entered the war on the British (and French) side.

60

The truly momentous nature of the entry of America on to the world stage could of course hardly have been perceived by the Allies. It was, hindsight confirms, a turning point in world history of massive proportions. The open involvement of a foreign power from three thousand miles away in the affairs of Europe – the mirror-image if you like of America's own history – needed a kind of ideological adjustment, or digestion, of some magnitude.

So far as Britain was concerned, the path of adjustment was clear. Americans were not savages. They were not Indians. They spoke our language.

And so, amidst much talk of 'Anglo-Saxon unity'; with messages of greeting involving 'a new and special heartiness' announced by Mr Winston Churchill from the people of Britain to the President of the United States; with the King, no less, scheduled to attend a special baseball match arranged in London between the US Army and Navy; with a meeting of the Anglo-Saxon Fellowship at Central Hall, Westminster (organized by the Minister of Information), graced by a 'short special prayer' from the Bishop of London, together with a long thundering editorial in *The Times* in support of what it called 'the old Anglo-Saxon "world idea"', the preparations for the celebration of American Independence Day ground out, in 1918, an unmistakable message. As Anglo-Saxons, speakers of English, freely embracing what amounted to their cultural destiny, if not duty, our fellow men, the Americans, would join us in combating the genuine savages, that race whose unspeakable activities and ineffable deformities marked them indelibly as men of Ind.

All nations execrate their enemies, and the discourse of denigration has a long and monotonous history in Europe, on all sides, and towards all cultural groups. But what is of interest at this turning point in European history is the mode and implication of a particular piece of vilification at a particular time. Academics, we could all profitably remember, are not exempt from this activity, and in fact are often rather good at it. Certainly the first Professor of English at Oxford University proved equal to the challenge. In the preface to a volume of lectures called *England and the War* published in 1918, Sir Walter Raleigh had observed that:

The character of Germany and the Germans is a riddle. . . . There is the same difficulty with the lower animals; our

61

description of them tends to be a description of nothing but our own loves and hates. Who has ever fathomed the mind of a rhinoceros?[14]

(pp. 7–8)

and in a lecture delivered on 14 March 1918 the same theme emerges:

That is what makes the Germans so like the animals. Their wisdom is all cunning. . . . You could talk to them about food, and they responded easily. It was all very restful and pleasant, like talking to an intelligent dog.

(ibid., p. 107)

Less than men, the Germans have a readily identifiable pattern of behaviour and the Professor speaks at length about

The filthiness that the Germans use, their deliberate befouling of all that is elegant and gracious and antique . . . their defiling with ordure the sacred vessels in the churches . . . a solemn ritual of filth, religiously practised, by officers no less than men.

(ibid., pp. 9–10)

Such animality in apparent human beings can only indicate savagery, and 'The waves of emotional exaltation which from time to time pass over the whole people have the same character, the character of savage religion' (p. 10). Germans are thus 'alien to civilization' and so to civilization's token, language: 'It is as if they despised language and made use of it only because they believe that it is an instrument of deceit' (p. 10). And as for the noises which amongst such sub-human creatures might have passed for language, here the Professor feels clearly called upon to make a dispassionate and objective professional assessment:

The Germans poisoned the wells in South-West Africa; in Europe they did all they could to poison the wells of mutual trust and mutual understanding among civilized men. Do they think that these things will make a good advertisement for the explosive guttural sounds and the huddled deformed syntax of the speech in which they express their arrogance and their hate?

(ibid., p. 93)

On 4 July 1918, then, the truth-bearing, civilizing and English-speaking representatives of humanity celebrated its confrontation with and certain defeat of its opposite, the savage, deformed, less than human representatives of the bestial and the depraved. Genuine men confronted creatures whose status was a matter of obvious dispute. English speakers, to change only the terms of the metaphor, confronted those whose animality was confirmed by their being deprived of that language.

Amongst the celebrations marking the day was an auspicious occasion all the more interesting since it wasn't formally part of the official celebrations. It was the occasion of the annual Shakespeare lecture of the British Academy. And that august body had chosen no less a person to address it than the Professor of English at Oxford University.

When of all people the Professor of English at Oxford University addresses of all bodies the British Academy on of all topics the subject of Shakespeare, then an audience might well feel that truths of a cardinal, possibly superlative, and certainly ultimate importance are likely to be delivered. Sir Walter Raleigh again proved equal to the occasion. Taking as his title 'Shakespeare and England', he produced, within that enormous range, a piece of ideological processing as perfectly fitted to the occasion as could be hoped. And at its centre, there is a reading of the scene from *The Tempest* with which this discussion began:

A small British expeditionary force, bound on an international mission, finds itself stranded in an unknown country. The force is composed of men very various in rank and profession. Two of them, whom we may call a non-commissioned officer and a private, go exploring by themselves, and take one of the natives of the place prisoner. This native is an ugly low-born creature, of great physical strength and violent criminal tendencies, a liar, and ready at any time for theft, rape, and murder. He is a child of Nature, a lover of music, slavish in his devotion to power and rank, and very easily imposed upon by authority. His captors do not fear him, and which is more, they do not dislike him. They found him lying out in a kind of no-man's land, drenched to the skin, so they determine to keep him as a souvenir, and to take him home with them. They nickname him, in friendly fashion, the monster, and the mooncalf, as who should say Fritz, or the Boche. But their first care is to give him a drink, and to make him swear allegiance upon the bottle.'Where the devil should he learn our language?', says the non-commissioned officer . . .

> (*Proceedings of the British Academy 1917–18*, pp. 407–8)

It is important that we should try to focus clearly on whatever is going on at this moment. In my view it has crucial implications, and it should not go unnoticed that Raleigh's sense of the occasion's importance is reflected in his subsequent printing of this lecture as the final item in the volume *England and the War*: a collection of which he said that if any of his books were to survive him, he believed that none had a better chance.[15]

Raleigh's aim – no cruder a project than that of many another critic – is, as I have said, to reinforce a particular ideological position at a vitally important historical conjuncture. The specificity of his reading at this point can be highlighted if we set it against a previous reading made by him some fourteen years earlier, in September 1904, just after he had accepted the Oxford chair. Writing then about *The Tempest* as a 'fantasy of the New World', he sees Trinculo not as a sturdy, good-natured 'non-commissioned officer', but quite the reverse: 'The drunken butler, accepting the worship and allegiance of Caliban, and swearing him in by making him kiss the bottle, is a fair representative of the idle and dissolute men who were shipped to the Virginian colony.' Similarly Caliban, far from being 'an ugly low-born creature, of great physical strength and violent criminal tendencies, a liar, and ready at any time for theft, rape, and murder', is seen as a 'wonderfully accurate' composition with 'his affectionate loyalty to the drunkard, his adoration of valour, his love of natural beauty and feeling for music and poetry' giving a clear manifestation of Shakespeare's 'sympathetic understanding' of uncivilized man.[16]

Both readings are of course partial, harshly reducing what we have readily recognized as the text's plurality to the dimensions of a single, coherent statement. But in the later, wartime one the ideological pressures work rather more obviously and their effects lie closer to the surface. In 1918, Caliban has to become less than a man in quite specific terms. He turns into a German, 'Fritz' or 'the Boche', a bestial, savage and deformed slave in a

precisely European dimension. Wholly determined, thus, as a
European 'wild man', as Peter Hulme's analysis has it, there is
clearly no room left in this reading of Caliban for any 'American'
potential. On 4 July 1918, this is self-evidently a good idea.

But more than that, the un-manning, the 'Germanizing' of
Caliban irons out any ambiguity that might accrue from his later
speaking of English. Any language that Caliban learns, is learned
for the purpose of cursing: the 'explosive guttural sounds and the
huddled deformed syntax of the speech' expressive of his nature.
What surfaces in this reading is something of genuine concern to
a Prospero-like Professor of English who is far more aware of
what is finally at stake than some of his later detractors have been
prepared to allow.

For what Raleigh clearly sees is that the war involves a historic
clash in terms of *linguistic* hegemony, and that victory in the
struggle would settle what, at that time, was a major issue: which
was to be the dominant world language, German or English? In a
letter to John Sampson on 6 July 1917, he had made his proph-
ecies crudely enough:

> The War is going to be All Right, my son. The English Language
> is safe to be the world language. The very Germans will treat
> their own tongue as a dialect. Goethe will be like Dunbar, or
> perhaps Burns. Scandinavians and Latins will cultivate English.
> German is a shotten herring. It's all right. . . . Their only chance
> was to bully their language up to a cock position, and they have
> failed. On its own merits it hasn't a chance.[17]

The entry of America into the war was portentous for this
reason. The 'special relationship' between Britain and the United
States was and is based on a common language, representing the
full flowering of the linguistic seeds planted by the Elizabethan
colonizers: a massive adventure in cultural re-creation to which
The Tempest stands as a lasting monument. By the time he
delivered a lecture entitled 'Some Gains of the War' to the Royal
Colonial Institute in February 1918, Raleigh was making it clear
that the major gain of American involvement in Europe would
surely be the subsequent dominance of Prospero's English over
Caliban's German: 'After the War the English language will have
such a position as it has never had before. It will be established in
world-wide security.' 'The future', it clearly follows, 'does not

belong to the German tongue' and it seems reasonable to announce that 'the greatest gain of all, the entry of America into the War assures the triumph of our common language'. English, and English men, will obviously be 'made' by such a victory – and the ambiguities lurking in that English verb gently surface as a curious fiscal metaphor seeps through the pseudo-philology:

> This gain, which I make bold to predict for the English language, is a real gain, apart from all patriotic bias. The English language is incomparably richer, more fluid, and more vital than the German language. Where the German has but one way of saying a thing, we have two or three, each with its distinctions and its subtleties of usage. Our capital wealth is greater, and so are our powers of borrowing.[18]

English, one might conclude, has scarcely ever been better served by those who profess it. It will become the gold standard, the sterling mark of civilization, the currency of sense, the mint of history, the hallmark of that which sets Prospero above Caliban, the common coin, in short, of genuine manhood.

Scarman

Happily, Sir Walter's account of the status of Germans proved open to a different audit. In his lecture 'The War and the Press' he goes on to make the comparatively sensible point that whatever the true nature of our enemies might be, it does not help the Allied cause if the newspapers persist in depicting *all* Germans as Calibans:

> Is it feared that we should have no heart for the War if once we are convinced that among the Germans there are some human beings? Is it believed that our people can be heroic on one condition only, that they shall be asked to fight no one but orang-outangs?[19]

This rather canny assessment of the function of propaganda was originally delivered to another bastion of the English establishment at Eton College on 14 March 1918. However, when Raleigh repeated it four months later at Mill Hill School in London, on 5 July, the day after the celebration of the American festivities, it was given a particular prominence in the next day's *Times*. It is an excellent indication of how constitutive contexts are of meaning that the lecture is now read by the *Times* reporter as outrageously extolling the virtues of our enemies. We cannot 'deny nobility', Raleigh is made to say, to the simple German soldier fighting for his country. Unfortunately, that is exactly what the discourse of the press was currently seeking to deny. The result, Raleigh tells us, was 'shoals of abusive letters by every post'; one of the worst from a working man who concluded by denying his manhood.[20] Worse was to follow. On 7 August, *The Times* reported a piece written in the German press by Raleigh's former colleague at Liverpool University, the 'notorious Professor Kuno Meyer'. Meyer (a scholar of Celtic) cleverly raised the spectre of further Calibans beyond the English pale by congratulating his old friend on the reported Mill Hill speech, and saying that his insight into the true nature of the German people undoubtedly came from the fact that Raleigh himself was not English, that Scottish blood ran in his veins, and that awareness of the Celtic dimension should undoubtedly make him applaud what Meyer, twisting the knife, calls the 'splendid behaviour' of the Irish rebels in Dublin in the rising of Easter 1916.

For the truth, revealed by these alternative readings, is that the world is not, shockingly, unitary or English in its meanings and does not always agree to be read as if it were. No doubt Kuno Meyer's ghost could find plenty of examples of subsequent 'splendid behaviour' in Ireland with which to undermine the current English reading of that particular tragic text.

Nor should we allow any notion of an 'essential' or 'stable' Shakespearian text, which can only be read in a particular way, to mock Sir Walter's shade. My point is not that he was engaged in any illicit importation into Shakespeare of extraneous political considerations in that, beyond those, there lies a comforting unchanging, permanent Shakespearian play to which we can finally turn. Shakespeare's texts always yield to, though they can never be reduced to, the readings we give them: their plurality makes Walter Raleighs of us all. As a result, his 1918 'politicized' reading of *The Tempest* is no isolated aberration. We should remind ourselves of the propaganda function of Olivier's film reading of *Henry V* (financed by government sources) which served as a prolegomenon to the D-Day landings in Normandy in 1944. We should remember E. M. W. Tillyard's *Shakespeare's History Plays* of the same period. And indeed, we can extend the process to the present day. One of the bizarre by-products of the Falklands campaign in 1982 was a book entitled *Authors Take Sides on the Falklands*. In it, the Shakespearian critic G. Wilson Knight delivers himself of the following:

> Britain's response to the Falklands crisis was ratified by all three parties in Parliament, and I accordingly would not presume to register any complaint. . . . I can only assess our prospects by stating my own convictions. I have for long accepted the validity of our country's historic contribution, seeing the British Empire as a precursor, or prototype, of world-order. I have relied always on the Shakespearian vision as set forth in my war-time production *This Sceptred Isle* at the Westminster Theatre in 1941 (described in *Shakespearian Production*, 1964). The theme I also discuss in various writings collected under the title *The Sovereign Flower* in 1958. Our key throughout is Cranmer's royal prophecy at the conclusion of Shakespeare's last play, *Henry VIII*, Shakespeare's final words to his countrymen. This I still hold to be our one authoritative statement, every word deeply significant, as forecast of the world-order at which we should aim.[21]

Shakespeare is a powerful ideological weapon, always available in periods of crisis, and used according to the exigencies of the time to resolve crucial areas of indeterminacy. As a central feature of the discipline we call 'English', his plays form part of that discipline's commitment – since 1870 in a national system of education – to the preservation and reinforcement of what is seen as a 'natural' order of things. To talk of a 'natural' order of things is of course to accept the limits imposed by the contours of a specific discourse. Such a discourse or 'knowledge' posits certain sets of differences or oppositions, presenting these as 'natural' and offering them for a variety of uses in response to historical pressures. My point is that the discourse forged by and for the Elizabethan colonial adventure offered a Prospero/Caliban, man/monster, non-Indian/Indian opposition of this sort which, since 1918 and Sir Walter Raleigh's astonishing reading of it, has made 'English-speaking/non-English-speaking' a feasible extension of its range. It involves the notion of one sort of English as the carrier and transmitter of the 'real' and the 'natural': the basis of that 'world-order' at which Wilson Knight chillingly urges us to aim. That English is the saving grace which is always denied to Caliban, but which must, in charity, always be offered to him. And it follows that those who reject, challenge or refuse that offer will find Caliban's mantle and fate ready and waiting for them.

Between 10 and 12 April 1981, it seemed to some in Britain as if Caliban had begun to take over the island. In the London district of Brixton, a series of violent incidents occurred which subsequently escalated to the level of a full-scale riot. Major participants were the Metropolitan police and those West Indian residents of the area whose presence perhaps represents one of the most ironic consequences of the Elizabethan encounter with the New World. After the event, the Government ordered an inquiry into the affair to be conducted by the Right Hon. the Lord Scarman, a High Court judge. His report is a model of what most people consider to be the essence of justice and good sense and its 'reading' of the disorders seems to have won general acceptance. Yet the basis of it is by now familiar: of the factors making the incorporation of the black community into the larger one extremely difficult, 'trouble with the English language' is seen as 'most important of all'. Not surprisingly, the central role of the study of English language and culture in promoting coherence and continuity becomes a constant theme: 'The problems which have to be solved, if deprivation and alienation are to be overcome, have been identified – namely, teaching a command of the English language, a broad education in the humanities, etc.'[22] More than a hundred years on, the spirit of the 1870 Education Act, mediated by Sir Walter Raleigh, glints purposefully through the text. 'While it is right', says Lord Scarman, speaking of the education of the immigrants' children,

> that the curriculum should fully recognize the value of different cultural traditions, I echo the Home Affairs Committee's view that the primary object of schooling must be to prepare all our children, whatever their colour, for life in Britain. It is essential, therefore, that children should leave school able to speak, read and write effectively in the language of British society, i.e. English.[23]

It is a minor, though not a carping point that the language of British society has never been, and is not now, simply English, and it is difficult to believe that a humane and learned British judge is genuinely unaware of that as a straightforward historical and social – not to say economic – fact. But then, in the face of what the report terms 'scenes of violence and disorder . . . the like of which had not previously been seen in this century in Britain' (p. 1); indeed, watching the flames spread with the outrageous symbolism Brixton affords – down Atlantic Road, into Chaucer Road, along Spenser Road, up Milton Road, ultimately to lick at the borders of Shakespeare Road itself – it becomes clear that the 'straightforward facts' can never be straightforwardly available to us, and that they present themselves only in the terms which a specific discourse permits, by routes which it lays down, streets which it names.

I have offered Sir Walter Raleigh's reading of *The Tempest* in support of this view, and it is only an extension of the same case to suggest that a version of the Prospero–Caliban conflict finds itself also located, indistinctly, intermittently, but nevertheless palpably, at a very deep level in the report of Lord Scarman.

Sir Walter's subsequent career manifests the rich rewards awaiting those whose readings, like those of Lord Scarman, find public favour. In the same month in which he gave his British Academy lecture, the Professor of English at Oxford found himself almost overtly 'made' in political terms: he was offered a seat in parliament by the Liberal prime minister, Asquith. Rejecting that dubious honour, he was nevertheless delighted to accept – in the same month – an appointment as official historian of the Royal Air Force, and, devoting the rest of his life to the task, managed to complete the first volume before his premature death in 1922.

As an example of another 'reading' and perhaps of a career which ended rather less auspiciously, I turn at last to Sir Walter Raleigh's illustrious namesake, who peers challengingly at us through the text of their common nomenclature. Since this intertextuality provides the only point of connection between the two (although the Elizabethan Sir Walter knew quite a lot about America, about Indians, and, on one famous occasion involving his cloak, the Queen and a muddy puddle, about prophylaxis), I offer a famous anecdote (that most revealing of texts) as a perfect instance of how, under the pressures of 'making', any use of language proves capable of disintegration. John Aubrey tells the story:

> He loved a wench well; and one time getting one of the Maids
> of Honour up against a tree in a wood ('twas his first lady) who

seemed at first boarding to be something fearful of her honour, and modest, she cried, 'Sweet Sir Walter, what do you me ask? Will you undo me? Nay, sweet Sir Walter! Sweet Sir Walter! Sir Walter!'. At last, as the danger and the pleasure at the same time grew higher, she cried in the ecstasy, 'Swisser Swatter, Swisser Swatter!'[24]

It remains a matter of only minor interest to record that the wench turned out eventually to be with child, that she was subsequently delivered of a son, and that a man was thus 'made' to the sound of this creative deconstruction of English letters.

Notes

1 Sidney Lee, 'The American Indian in Elizabethan England', in F. S. Boas (ed.), *Elizabethan and Other Essays* (London, Oxford University Press, 1929), 263–301.
2 ibid., 292.
3 Peter Hulme, 'Hurricanes in the Caribbees: the constitution of the discourse of English colonialism' in Francis Barker *et al.* (eds), *1642: Literature and Power in the Seventeenth Century* (Colchester, University of Essex, 1981), 55–83. Compare Frank Kermode, introduction to the Arden edition of *The Tempest* (London, 1954), xxxviii ff., and J. E. Hankins, 'Caliban the Bestial Man', PMLA LXII (1947), 793 ff.
4 Kermode, op. cit., xxiv.
5 G. M. Trevelyan, *English Social History* (London, 1942), 581.
6 K. M. Elisabeth Murray, *Caught in the Web of Words* (New Haven and London, 1977), 340.
7 D. J. Palmer, *The Rise of English Studies* (Oxford and Hull, 1965), 112 ff. There had been previous chairs of English at Oxford, but the main concern of their holders was philological. The new chair was not filled until the death of the Merton professor, John Earle, in 1904.
8 Simon Nowell-Smith (ed.), *Letters to Macmillan* (London, 1967), 162–4.
9 John Gross, *The Rise and Fall of the Man of Letters* (London, 1969); Penguin edn (Harmondsworth, 1973), 122–3.
10 *Letters to Macmillan*, 163.
11 ibid., 250.
12 Walter Raleigh, *Letters* (2 vols), ed. Lady Raleigh (London, 1926), 1, 253, 259. Aspects of Raleigh's career at Oxford are discussed in Chris Baldick, *The Social Mission of English Criticism* (Oxford, 1983), 75–92. For an admiring account of Raleigh's qualities as a teacher see Stephen Potter, *The Muse in Chains* (London, 1937), 202–18.
13 Raleigh, *Letters*, 1, 128–9.

14 Walter Raleigh, *England and the War* (Oxford, Clarendon Press, 1918).
15 Raleigh, *Letters*, 1, xvii.
16 Walter Raleigh, 'The English Voyages of the Sixteenth Century', in Richard Hakluyt, *The Principal Navigations, Voyages, Traffiques and Discoveries of the English Nation* (1589), 12 vols (Glasgow, James MacLehose, 1905), XII, 112–13.
17 Raleigh, *Letters*, II, 468.
18 Raleigh, *England and the War*, 93–5.
19 ibid., 118.
20 Raleigh, *Letters*, II, 488.
21 C. Woolf and J. Moorcroft Wilson (eds), *Authors Take Sides on the Falklands* (London, Woolf, 1982), 66–7.
22 *The Brixton Disorders 10–12 April, 1981* (Scarman Report) (London, HMSO, 1981), 9–10.
23 ibid., 105.
24 *Brief Lives*, MS Aubrey 6, fol. 77. Cit. Norman Lloyd Williams, *Sir Walter Raleigh* (London, 1962), 88–9.

4

That Shakespeherian Rag

Play

'O,O,O,O' – not echoes of Sir Walter Raleigh's further escapades but, according to the Folio text, the last utterance of the Prince of Denmark. The rest there is certainly not silence, but whatever range of noises and movements an actor might summon in response to these disturbing printer's signs. No doubt they represent several harrowing seconds of action on the stage, and Horatio's subsequent 'Now cracks a noble heart' (V. ii. 364) perhaps supplies an appropriate commentary on their boisterousness.

Yet any account of the critical processing of Shakespeare's plays has to come to terms with the fact that the editors of *Hamlet* almost unanimously suppress these moments. Stigmatized as an 'actor's interpolation', the Prince's terminal 'O's find themselves sternly banished from the text: an odd verdict, it might be concluded, on what could otherwise rank as a perceptive gloss on the part by its first and rather astute critic, the actor Richard Burbage.

Hamlet might be presented after all as a man who has struggled mightily to retain in his language something of the humanity that has been debased and debilitated by the actions of his 'mighty opposite' in the Danish court. That we should witness speech itself finally and violently vanquished in him, hear that probing voice reduced at last to groaning, recognize in those 'O's the fearful

73

linguistic and therefore cultural consequences of Claudius's poison, could become powerful aspects of the play's statement. If this is interpolation, we might be tempted to say, give us excess of it.

The editorial exasperation induced by Hamlet's groaning thus requires some explanation. Why this conspiracy to expunge the Prince's agony in the name of textual scholarship? One answer possibly lies in the notion of the 'text' and its nature that such scholarship seems to presuppose.

Text

The case of A. C. Bradley indicates the kind of problems that the quest for a perfectly expressive text generates for a particular sort of criticism. Modern textual scholarship pursues a similar quarry: an originary, coherent body of written material, the full expression of an author's thought, to which the text assembled by the scholar aims to approximate in fact or spirit. Fredson Bowers, one of the founding fathers of the approach, describes its programme succinctly. In respect of Shakespeare, such scholarship, he tells us, 'has only one object: to recover as nearly as may be, in the most minute detail, precisely what Shakespeare wrote, both in content and in form'.[1] The idea of an authoritative body of material, 'what Shakespeare wrote', whose authority resides in the fact of its unmediated derivation from the springs of its author's invention, beckons like a Holy Grail beyond the tactics designed for its recovery. If the central concern of textual criticism is to establish 'the nature and authority of texts', then, Bowers continues, 'a critic "recovers" Shakespeare's text most notably by identifying those documents in which the texts are preserved in their most authoritative form and rejecting all other versions that have had no access to fresh authority'.[2] As a result, the modern weapons of textual scholarship enable us to 'strip the veil of print from a text and thus to recover a number of the precise details of the underlying manuscript'.[3]

Such metaphors covertly map a familiar conceptual terrain. Buried treasure glints: here be dragons. The printed text 'veils' an 'underlying' manuscript, its sacramental status guaranteed by the fact that it issues literally from the hand of the author. From this origin, a controlling God-like authority (linked with the term 'author') ultimately descends. And this demands – indeed authorizes – the 'recovery' of those pristine, unsullied, authoritative words which languish now buried, soiled and distorted by print. The hint of a moral, not to say religious imperative peeps out, matched by the promise of scholarly derring-do. As the editorial task-force embarks, we might notice that the Bible, aptly enough, offers a relevant model in respect of its own scriptures: 'for until this day remaineth the same vail untaken away in the reading of the old testament; which vail is done away in Christ. . . . Nevertheless when it shall turn to the Lord, the vail shall be taken away' (2 *Corinthians* 3: 14–16). Pursuit of the original word of God may indeed join in some minds with pursuit of the original word of the Bard. But apart from the fact that no manuscripts of Shakespeare's plays have so far come to light, the main project adumbrated here must be doomed to failure, since it aims to circumvent what in truth can never be circumvented: the process of mediation. Even if we allow, in the terms of the misleading metaphor, that the printed text indeed mediates the 'underlying' manuscript, that manuscript itself can only be a mediation (to follow the metaphor through) of the no less 'underlying' thought that generates its words. And thought can hardly avoid the mediation which casts it in linguistic form any more than the variety of experiences which 'underlie' thought can avoid the mediation of the social and political context in which they must occur, and so on. We can have no access to anyone's 'original' or unmediated apprehensions, let alone Shakespeare's. And if to write these down subjects them to mediation, then to read them can only further mediate the already mediated. In the case of printed plays of the sixteenth and seventeenth centuries a whole array of additional agencies interposes itself willy-nilly: copyists, scribes, reporters. And even if we could push all these aside, that still fails to guarantee the innocence or purity of the scholar's view, for that itself imports unthinkingly into the process all the presuppositions that go with the modern concept of professional scholarship.

Certainly, the notion of a single 'authoritative' text, immediately expressive of the plenitude of its author's mind and meaning, would have been unfamiliar to Shakespeare, involved as he was in the collaborative enterprise of dramatic production, and notoriously unconcerned to preserve in stable form the texts of most of his plays. A project which seeks to award those texts the status of holy writ, to bind them to their origins and to cleanse from them the alien and sullying 'interpolations' of such as Richard Burbage, has a worryingly unacknowledged modern air: the product of a culture which characteristically invests a good deal of intellectual capital in concepts of individuality, originality, personal ownership and responsibility, and maintains a high regard for the printed text as a personal unmediated statement, particularly in the form of 'literature'. If the model for this latter concept can be said to be the novel, then its application to the texts of Shakespeare's plays imposes on them the presuppositions of that genre: it turns them into quasi-novels, by requiring of them the same kind of reductive author-centred 'authenticity', forever haunted by the spectre of interpolation.

Play-text

An alternative must lie in a response to the full implications of the Shakespearian texts that confront us and in an attempt to give their textuality full rein. They constitute, after all, something that our available textual categories currently require us to think of as hybrid. They are not novels. They are not plays. They are not poems.

They are, of course, play-texts. However, that scandalously indeterminate status invites recuperation, and this has tended to take the form of determined programmes of critical processing in the interests of one or other neighbouring categories. Well-known mutations result, for example:

1 The play-text as novel. Here the critic approaches the play-text as if it were a work of fiction in the 'realistic' mode. As we have seen in the case of A. C. Bradley, this approach encourages a sense of being able to go 'through' the text to a 'real world' lying beyond it, to which the text offers direct, unmediated access. That reality is guaranteed by the author's presence, for it expresses his 'point of view' through the activities of almost-live characters. The reader reads the play-text in order to reach that reality.

2 The play-text as play. This view also sees the play-text as referring to a 'reality' lying beyond it. However, in this case

76

that 'reality' consists of an actual play, realized on the stage. The action on the stage has priority, and the text serves a secondary role as a kind of 'score' for the performance. In this sense the text functions less as a window on to the reality beyond than as a kind of nagging, admonitory signpost which points the reader away from itself. The performed play can be thought to follow, or to 'score off' the score according to the 'point of view' the director (who becomes a kind of author in the process) is concerned to promote.

3 The play-text as poem. Here the play-text finds itself presented, neither as a window on to a further reality, nor as a signpost or score in relation to a realized play-on-the-stage, but more as a self-referring verbal structure almost in the mode of a symbolist poem. It exhibits patterns, deploys themes, points to itself, and takes itself as its ultimate subject.

Quite clearly, each of these approaches seeks to recuperate the play-text on behalf of a tried and trusted genre, and to limit its potential accordingly. None of them takes account of the degree of unclassifiable – and so threatening – productivity which the play-text disconcertingly offers to release, as a result of the tension it maintains between the various modes of reading that aim to process it. As the site of competition between different ways of reading, the play-text stands, not as a different kind of text, but as the occasion which calls into question some of our presuppositions concerning the activity of reading all texts. That is its value.

Of course, each of the recuperative strategies mentioned above has its own arguments for removing such play-textual events as Hamlet's 'O's. If the play-text is seen as a window-like novel, then the usual 'ordering' processes required by the appropriate conventions will domesticate those 'O's by subsuming them completely into what we already know, and turning them into mere superfluities in respect of that knowledge. They tell us that Hamlet is dying, that he is in pain. Since the 'real' words, the actual lexical items of the text, have already told us as much, the 'O's are redundant and may be cut.

If the play-text is seen as a score or signpost whose only genuine and acceptable realization takes the form of action on the stage, then Hamlet's 'O's become mere 'shorthand' indications for the

director or actor, suggesting a certain range of action and concomitant verbal sound. The response to this suggestion remains
none the less a matter for the director and the demands of the
particular 'interpretation' at stake, to be promulgated at the
expense of these or, notoriously, almost any other signals the
play-text may offer. Once again, the 'O's risk redundancy, or
cutting.

If, finally, the play-text is treated as an opaque, intrinsically
coherent, self-reflexive thematic structure, then of course the
'O's can be moulded to fit that structure, and given the kind of de-
fusing, normalizing reading offered above. They become part of
the 'theme' of language and its relation to humanity, and of the
destruction of humanity that the destruction of language involves. And as mere exemplars of that already established
thematic structure – albeit moving and ingenious ones – they
serve primarily to reinforce what the text has said before and
perhaps need not say again at this point: in short, once more, they
are redundant.

Only when we step outside these stratagems does the spectre of
redundancy recede. And when that happens, a dimension
beyond those already touched on comes into view. Immediately
it overwhelms any 'normalizing' or domesticating reading,
because Hamlet's 'O's lead us to the boundaries of experience
and offer to push us beyond them. They invite us to 'read'
another person's final, engulfing agony and follow his headlong
plunge into an area about which we can have no 'normalizing'
knowledge or experience, one from which no traveller returns.
Beyond words themselves, those 'O's threaten to pull the
linguistic rug from under our feet. At this moment the conventions of normal reading, normal expectation, normal modes
of signification (to read in a normal way is to assert normality)
find themselves at risk. As the text apparently disintegrates, the
play-text, fully activated, comes into its own. Offering to break
the reader's domesticating grip, it ceases to function as the
passive raw material we habitually process as novel, play or
poem. Instead, in the breakdown of that processing which it
engineers and fosters, it involves the reader in a catastrophe to
match Hamlet's own. In other words the printer's conventional
sign, 'O' for agony, turns convention on its head here by forcing
on to the text a disturbing mode of communication. It works,

wordlessly, to subvert words, and to drain our intellectual investment from them just as, in its character as 'paralanguage' (to use
G. L. Trager's term), it subverts the very structure and presuppositions of written language itself.[4] We encounter at such
moments, and they are the moments which systematically
characterize the play-text and make it distinctive, the enormous
capacity for the generation of meaning inherent in that non-
discursive, musical or 'tonal' dimension of language, for which
'paralanguage' lamely stands. It is one for which, as students of
English, we have no adequate critical vocabulary.

O play that thing

T. S. Eliot is not reckoned amongst the great Shakespearian
critics. His failure with *Hamlet* has been seen as both notable and
typical in that, not being English, he seems unable to grasp the
play's links with a native, English tradition.[5] The mind that had
'never . . . seen a cogent refutation of Thomas Rymer's objections
to *Othello*' finds *Hamlet* 'most certainly an artistic failure' and
'full of some stuff that the writer could not drag to light, contem-
plate or manipulate into art'. Moreover, he admits that this
'feeling' is 'very difficult to localize. You cannot point to it in the
speeches.' The essence of the play seems in fact to lie 'beyond'
the words which appear to embody it in the text, in what he was
careful to call its 'unmistakable tone'.[6]

The use of paralinguistic features of language, and in particular
'tone', as part of a deliberate communicative strategy was always
crucial to Eliot's own verse, as indeed to the whole symbolist
enterprise.[7] It is a quality which resides in the intonational
context in which words are uttered, and the manner of their
voicing, over and above their overt meaning. Its function in
language is of course central, because it serves to produce
meaning in concrete situations through the assertion of values,
political positions, points of view. In recent years it has become
clear that Mikhail Bakhtin's work makes the complexities of
paralanguage and their involvement in utterance the basis of his
'dialogic' conception of language. For Bakhtin, language never
occurs in the abstract. It always represents an intervention into a
continuing dialogue, and its meanings constitute and are constituted by a response to that context of utterance. Paralinguistic

intonation thus forms a central feature of the process by which meaning is generated. As Katerina Clark and Michael Holquist put it, 'Utterance is an activity that enacts differences in values . . . the same words can mean different things depending on the particular intonation with which they are uttered in a specific context: intonation is the sound that value makes.'[8] As an American, particularly one concerned to establish himself in an English context and to embrace and influence English values, Eliot might be expected to exhibit considerable paralinguistic sensitivity in the matter of 'the sound that value makes'. His politic transformation of his own native American accent into an upper-class English one must rank as one of the heroic dialogic feats of our century, one well capable of reinforcing the sense any alien has that the 'fit' between the 'realities' of language, culture and experience can never be the seamless, effortless, inevitable matter for the immigrant that it is for the native. Constituting as it does a good deal of the ultimate achievement both of Eliot's life and his verse, the element of 'tone' becomes the factor to which he responds with most sensitivity in the work of Shakespeare.

Of course, the concept of 'tone' also has a melodic dimension, aptly suggestive of the power of non-discursive musical sound to penetrate the heart and brain. And the 'tonal' combination of words and music in popular song, together with the capacity of that combination literally to invade, to 'catch' our apprehensions and to take them over, is intentionally hinted at in the title of this chapter; a phrase that, however unlikely it may be to record the fact, nevertheless constitutes one of the most memorable links between two of the most influential writers in English: a wry 'tonal' acknowledgement perhaps, from the centre of a modern American text towards one of its author's English masters.

It would be uncharacteristic if it were not also fairly acute. And when we turn again to 'The Waste Land', we discover that at least one of the levels of irony implicit in that acknowledgement inheres in its knowing 'play-text'-like use of the same printer's sign, 'tonally', paralinguistically conceived, that we have already encountered: 'O O O O that Shakespeherian Rag'.

It will come as no surprise to those with a taste for Eliotic humour to learn that there really was such a song, as B. R. McElderry has pointed out.[9] The work of the almost eponymous

team of Gene Buck and Herman Ruby (words) and David
Stamper (music), 'That Shakespearian Rag', with its chorus

> That Shakespearian rag
> Most intelligent, very elegant,
> That old classical drag,
> Has the proper stuff, the line 'Lay on Macduff'

was one of the hit numbers of 1912, a year which offered it
considerable competition in the shape of 'Everybody's Doin' It'
and 'Be My Little Baby Bumble Bee'. Interestingly enough, its
success was positively identified, in the advertisements promoting the song, with its live performance. In *Variety* for 25 October of
that year, it was billed as 'Roy Samuels' big hit in *Ziegfield's Follies
of 1912'*, and the song's publishers, listing it fourth among ten
titles in a *Variety* advertisement for 19 July of the same year added,
'If you want a song that can be acted as well as sung send for this
big surprise hit.' The song's title uses the term 'Shakespearian'.
Eliot's 'interpolation' of the extra syllable in 'Shakespeherian',
and his addition of the 'O's (which do not occur in the printed text),
confirm and reinforce a 'tonal' dialogic dimension that obviously
struck him as wholly appropriate (and indeed has turned out to be
efficacious: line 128 of 'The Waste Land' has preserved the song's
banality far more effectively than the performance of Mr
Samuels). The whole episode indicates a subtlety of ear, a
sensitivity to actual performance, utterance, and intonation, and a
degree of paralinguistic acuity that is distinctive.

It was an ear that recognized its own capabilities in Shakespeare. In a broadcast talk on John Dryden (published in the
Listener, 22 April 1931, pp. 681–2) in which he compares parallel
passages from *All for Love* and *Antony and Cleopatra*, Eliot had
offered a precise instance. It concerns the death of Charmian.[10]

North's translation of Plutarch gives the following account of
Charmian's last words: 'One of the soldiers seeing her, angrily
sayd unto her: Is that well done, Charmion? Verie well sayd she
againe, and meet for a Princes descended from the race of so
many noble kings.'[11]

Dryden's version of this is

> Yes, 'tis well done, and like a Queen, the last
> Of her great race: I follow her. (*Sinks down and dies*)
>
> (V. i)

81

Shakespeare's version is

> It is well done, and fitting for a princess,
> Descended of so many royal kings.

– and then he adds the two words

> Ah, soldier!

(V. ii. 325–7)

before she dies.

Eliot's comment on the difference between these versions indicates his recognition of the remarkable nature of Shakespeare's play-text. You cannot, he argues, 'say that the two lines of Dryden are either less poetic than Shakespeare's, or less dramatic'. The difference lies in the 'remarkable addition' to the original text of North: the 'two plain words, ''Ah, soldier'''. Eliot finds himself nonplussed by the inexplicable effect these words have on him, and he recognizes it as a feature of the play-text itself:

> there is nothing in them for the actress to express in action; she can at best enunciate them clearly. I could not myself put into words the difference I feel between the passage if these two words, 'Ah, soldier', were omitted and with them. But I know there is a difference, and that only Shakespeare could have made it.

(*Listener*, p. 681)

The difference is the more remarkable perhaps because of the deliberation with which it has been manufactured. North's Plutarch proves both explicit and emphatic in ending Charmian's words where Dryden leaves them, even adding 'She sayd no more; but fell down dead hard by the bed.' What Shakespeare introduces, and what Eliot finds himself ineluctably respondent to are two words in which the essential features of what we have been calling the play-text seem to reside.

Eliot's account falls short only in its suggestion that there is nothing in these words that can be expressed in action. For this underestimates a fundamental relationship of words to action that *Antony and Cleopatra* can be said fully to exploit.

After all, nobody just talks: communication normally draws on a complex interaction between voice and body, sound and gesture.[12]

At one level, *Antony and Cleopatra* focuses on two flawed worlds in which that necessary, humanizing interdependency has ceased to operate. Voice dominates the Roman world; body that of Egypt. If Rome is a place of words, Egypt is a place of actions. Rome's auditory, temporal world, where love is talked of, thus proves as incomplete as Egypt's visual, spatial world, where love is made.

Antony accordingly finds himself committed to and limited by a way of life in which body rules voice. And his commitment signals itself directly in the play's first scene, in an appropriately wordless, iconic moment. 'Kingdoms are clay', he announces,

> The nobleness of life
> Is to do thus
>
> (I. i. 35–7)

– whereupon he turns and kisses Cleopatra.

The importance of this gesture to the play's concerns can be judged from the risk it evidently takes of embarrassing or distracting an audience aware that on this stage male actors normally took the parts of women. Like most contemporary dramatists, Shakespeare rarely encourages much physical contact on stage between men and 'women' for this reason. The memorable reference on Cleopatra's part to the fact that her own greatness might be 'boyed' in the Roman streets (V. ii. 218–20), together with other frequent reminders that 'she' is male, serve to focus an 'alienated' and so powerfully reiterated attention on this physical aspect of her relationship with Antony throughout the play.

In short, that moment when their bodies unite on the stage turns out to be centrally significant. The word 'thus' read in its full playtextual sense, and in the light of its accompanying gesture, signifies a catastrophically physical way of life committed to communication primarily through and with the body. The beds in the east are soft, and the intensest kind of wordless bodily communion prevails there. Cleopatra's own person proves word-defeating: it beggars all descriptions, and both she and her attendants tend to use language itself less as a vehicle for rational discourse than as a physically luxurious entity. Even a surprised messenger finds himself urged alarmingly to

> Ram thou thy fruitful tidings in mine ears,
> That long time have been barren.
>
> (II. v. 24–5)

83

In this context, Antony's death presents itself in appropriately sensual, sexual terms: he resolves to be

> A bridegroom in my death, and run into't
> As to a lover's bed.
>
> (IV. xiv. 100–1)

And he ends in that vein by falling on his sword, reiterating to the aptly named Eros that recurrent playtextual signal of catastrophe,

> To do thus
> I learnt of thee.
>
> (IV. xiv. 102–3)

Of course there is an apt pun on 'death' (in the sense of sexual climax) which the play exploits at length both here and throughout. In a world where the 'nobleness of life' resides in 'doing thus' with such frequency, Enobarbus's commentary on Cleopatra's 'celerity in dying' – her response to the 'mettle in death' (I. ii. 143 ff.) – has a double edge. It is wholly appropriate, then, that at the play's end she should speak of 'immortal longings' in her own body, discover that

> The stroke of death is as a lover's pinch
> Which hurts, and is desir'd
>
> (V. ii. 294–5)

and so generate the pun's final explicit irony. A life based on 'doing thus' as its sole end finds nothing at its conclusion but a grimmer and more final version of the 'death' it has punningly pursued all along. Cleopatra's physical death becomes the fitting 'climax' of her many sexual 'deaths'. Induced by the fondled, phallic asp, it has, properly, an orgasmic dimension, overt, yet subversive of normal linguistic structures:

> As sweet as balm, as soft as air, as gentle –
> O Antony!
>
> (V. ii. 310–11)

When Charmian dies, shortly afterwards, that body-dominated world of 'doing thus' finally dies – in every sense – with her. For her 'Ah, soldier' matches her mistress's 'O Antony' and signals, indeed constitutes, its death-knell. In that capacity it bespeaks an appropriate and orgasmic last gesture from the male actor, fully suggestive of the pun on death, by whose means the uncomprehending Roman soldier, and the world of mere words he represents, is wordlessly, paralinguistically, tonally mocked.

In short, just as Hamlet's paralinguistic 'O's indicated, through their subversion of standard lexical structures, the inadequacies of domesticating reading when this confronts the catastrophe of death, so Charmian's paralinguistic 'Ah, soldier' promotes a similar kind of subversion, involves us in a similar sense of catastrophe, in a death whose disturbing links with sexual climax have been the occasion of a good deal of preparatory punning. Eliot's emphasis on this moment of the play-text sufficiently indicates his sense of its importance. And of course his mock bewilderment in the face of it, 'I could not myself put into words the difference I feel', has its own paralinguistic dialogical role to play. For the declaration of the breakdown of his own normalizing reading here gives his account of this moment a powerful playtextual dimension which finally sweeps away argument and offers simply to engulf us in what he thinks of as the essence of Shakespeare's art.

All that jouissance

The recent revival of interest in classical ragtime music has placed it in quite a different perspective from that encouraged by the users of the word 'ragtime' in the years following the First World War, when an attempt was made to link it with the emergent, challenging music of black America in the form of the blues and jazz. In fact, ragtime represents a quite different, opposite mode. Essentially a *written* music, the classical ragtime composers insist that it should be played *as written* on the piano. Its bearing fundamentally opposes that of the blues and of jazz, in that it represents a 'writing-down' of the orality which blues and jazz promote. Its whole import suggests the reverse of the black, the improvisatory and the African. It constitutes a bid on the part of its early (and best) exponents for genteel, white, European respectability. Its aim is to be both 'elegant' and 'intelligent', and the monuments to this endeavour lie in the two ill-fated ragtime operas, *A Guest of Honour* (1903) and *Treemonisha* (1911), by the black ragtime composer Scott Joplin (1868–1917).

After Sedalia, Missouri, whose Maple Leaf Café is commemorated in Joplin's enormously popular 'Maple Leaf Rag' (1899), the great formative centre of ragtime was the town of St Louis in the same state. Joplin himself moved there in 1900; the lost *A Guest of Honour* achieved its single recorded performance there in 1903. And in 1904 the city was host to a National Ragtime Contest. Of course, St Louis was and is not unknown for its connection with the great native American art – ragtime's opposite – the blues. And so anyone with any connection with St Louis in those years (and Eliot's was close enough for him to make an unwarranted, but clearly deeply felt and embarrassing reference in later years to his own paralinguistic, dialogic relationship with the city of his birth; his 'nigger drawl')[13] would have encountered head on the plainly opposed polarities of native American music: on the one hand the written texts of ragtime, on the other the orality of blues and jazz that ragtime specifically denied.

On another level, such a polarization could be said to be of a fundamental order. It represents perhaps, in miniature, the sort of unresolved dichotomy that, experienced as indicative of a deeper rift, or raised to a higher symbolic power, might ultimately lay waste any culture: deny it, in terms of Eliot's later vision, the cohesion whose absence 'The Waste Land' and much of his critical enterprise laments.

Ironically, the presumed embodiment of that presupposed cohesion, the plays of Shakespeare, have found themselves over the centuries forced into the service of a similar cultural dichotomy. From a position as a major instance of English-speaking popular culture, they have over 400 years dwindled to become the exemplars of internationally revered high art. From their function as an oral externalization of the tensions within their own culture, they have shrunk to be sacred written texts; their guardians, from Dr Johnson on, ever eager to expunge from their pages the betraying signs of orality. 'A dramatic exhibition', Johnson thunders, in his *Preface to the Plays of William Shakespeare* (1765), 'is a book recited with concomitants that increase or diminish its effect.' If 'Familiar comedy is often more powerful on the theatre than in the page; imperial tragedy is always less. . . . A play read affects the mind like a play acted.'

It is worth checking our risibility for the moment to reflect that the Johnsonian voice, ever ready to excise or 'blot' from

Shakespeare's 'book' such 'forced and unnatural metaphors' as may fail, *inter alia*, to match the requirements of *written* sense, still makes itself heard in the land. As we have seen in respect of Hamlet's 'O's, labels as confident in their presuppositions as 'intrusive matter', 'actor's interpolations', 'stage accretions' deriving from 'corruption through performance' remain the common coin of one kind of textual scholarship.[14]

But 'intrusive' *into* what? 'accretions' *on to* what? 'corruptions' *of* what? The point bears repetition: there is no pristine manu-script of any of Shakespeare's plays. And even if there were, on what basis would we grant it stronger authority than, say, the text of a prompt-book which relates, with some immediacy, to an actual contemporary performance in which the author's acqui-escence was not improbable?[15] Those who, seeking to make the plays 'elegant' and 'intelligent', speak slightingly of actors' 'inter-polations' in them might remember that Shakespeare himself was an actor.

We are dealing, after all, when we speak of play-texts, with constructs whose form makes them subversive. They are neither simply novels, nor simply poems or plays: they stand outside – and thus call into question – the only categories we have available to describe them.

Indeed, if we agree with Claude Lévi-Strauss that 'impoverish-ment and mutilation' lie in wait for particular aspects of orality at the level of the written word, then the model for the language of the play-text, for what he calls the 'language which transcends the level of articulated language', must obviously and more precisely be located elsewhere.[16]

The link between drama and music lies of course in the element of performance. And no reader of Eliot can fail to feel at home with Lévi-Strauss's account of the musical process: 'In listening to music – and while we are listening – we have achieved a kind of immortality. . . . The music lives out its life in me; I listen to myself through the music.'[17] In Eliot's words (from the aptly named *Four Quartets*) this becomes

> music heard so deeply
> That it is not heard at all, but you are the music
> While the music lasts.
>
> ('The Dry Salvages')

The sense of 'being' the performance can of course pervade audiences of both music and drama. In fact, music offers actively to involve itself with the regular pulse of our bodies. Its rhythms seem to invite a participatory, dialogical response from, and finally almost reach out to catch, the independent rhythms of our nervous systems. Perhaps we call melodies 'catchy' as a result. Eliot's own symbolist verse works in a similar fashion, invading the mind paralinguistically, burrowing as he puts it 'below the conscious levels of thought and feeling'.

The essence of that native American musical tradition, ragtime's opposite, blues and jazz, lies in a similar process: in its reaching out to and invasion of its listener's being 'below the conscious levels of thought and feeling', in the identification with the performance that it demands from an audience, and in the identity it insists on between performance and performer: a performance in which 'interpolations' in and on to the original 'text' or sequence of chords literally constitute the music and make the player, music and audience simultaneously part of the same momentary whole.

In the form of qualities which cannot be 'dragged to light', which you cannot 'point to in the speeches', but which, as in Hamlet's 'O,O,O,O' or Charmian's 'Ah, soldier', or Antony's 'thus', exhibit an involving and implicating musical power beyond ordinary words, these are the fundamental characteristics of the play-text that Eliot perceptively recognized as 'unmistakable' in Shakespeare. To respond adequately to the productivity of these moments is to recognize their tonal, dialogic involvement with paralanguage and to condone their consequent loosening of the signifier–signified ligaments whose network usually seems to determine the boundaries of meanings within which the play operates.

Once that happens, once that anaesthetic lifts, the play-text reaches out for the reader. And even if, as a defensive measure, we seek to impose a limiting, analgesic, domesticating meaning upon the event – 'Ah, soldier' 'means' orgasm, 'O,O,O,O' 'means' agony and death, 'thus' 'means' a commitment to a way of life – and even when we try to link these meanings, as I have suggested we might, with the larger 'thematic' contours of each play, we still have not disposed of them, nor can we. For their range of signification extends beyond the frontiers of language, and so of experience as we know it. However ingeniously 'explained', those 'ah's and 'O's and 'thus's continue to subvert order, to disrupt sequence, to impede the linear flow of meaning because that is what their final referents – orgasm, disintegration, despair and death – finally do. To attempt a 'normalizing' reading of them simply highlights the inadequacy of an inherited normality in the face of its abandonment which they represent. In effect, 'normal reading' itself, with all its implications, is precisely what they have abandoned. As a result, they offer an orthographical blank, a vacancy, a disconcerting sign which invites a dialogical 'improvised' response. Each one constitutes a point at which, to use Roland Barthes's terms, the garment of predictable, expected content provocatively and disturbingly gapes, and the play-text reaches out and draws us irresistibly towards itself and the *jouissance* or *jazz* (is there a philological connection between these terms?) which it promises.[18]

Colla voce

At these moments, perhaps, the realms of music (particularly improvised jazz music) and play-text combine, to produce what Barthes has called the paradox of 'writing aloud'. Its nature, he says, is not phonemic (i.e. meaningful) but phonetic (involving pure verbal sound):

> its aim is not the clarity of messages . . . what it searches for (in a perspective of bliss [*jouissance*]) are the pulsional incidents, the language lined with flesh, a text where we can hear the grain of the throat, the patina of consonants, the voluptuousness of vowels, a whole carnal stereophony: the articulation of the body, of the tongue, not that of meaning, of language.

He adds that 'a certain art of singing can give an idea of this vocal writing'.[19]

Eliot's lifelong interest in vocalization needs little demonstration. The typescript of the early drafts of 'The Waste Land' shows a distinctive oral bearing. Full of demotic utterances (the first part of the poem in this version is entitled 'He Do The Police in Different Voices') it is also studded with snatches of popular songs. And when Eliot transferred himself to England and undertook a massive development of his own 'voicing' of the language on a personal as well as a public level, this interest in 'vocal writing' persisted in the form of his frequentation of popular music-halls.

He was probably thinking more of his own problems as a playwright than of Shakespeare when, writing of the 'moral superiority' of the greatest British music-hall star of her day, he pointed out that

> The working man who went to the music-hall and saw Marie Lloyd, and joined in the chorus, was himself performing part of the act; he was engaged in that collaboration of the audience with the artist which is necessary in all art and most obviously in dramatic art.[20]

But that creative 'collaboration' clearly constitutes a good deal of what he thought of as the genuine Shakespearian playtextual 'music' – demeaned by the exploitative vulgarity (and, incidentally, wholly mistaken musical assumptions) of Messrs Buck, Ruby and Stamper's 'Shakespearian Rag'.

Being an American helped him to recognize something that Bradley, being English, missed: the sound of the human voice and the demand for dialogue, for joining in the chorus, that it embodies. Only Coleridge, that least English of English critics, has put it better. Speaking of Shakespeare he says, 'You feel him to be a poet inasmuch as for a time he has made you one – an active, creative being.'[21] In short, like all texts in which dialogic 'voicing' or tonality is crucial (like the blues, like the singing of Marie Lloyd) Shakespeare's play-texts – that Shakespeherian Rag – reach out to us (as it were with that extra, dialogical syllable), invade us and invite us to make (with that paralinguistic 'O,O,O,O') a sympathetic act of closure with themselves. And as the groaning Burbage knew, that turns us, even as we read, from spectators into participants.

Notes

1 Fredson Bowers, 'Textual criticism' in O. J. Campbell and E. G. Quinn (eds), *The Reader's Encyclopedia of Shakespeare* (New York, 1966), 864.

2 ibid., 865.

3 ibid., 869.

4 G. L. Trager, 'Paralanguage: a first approximation', *Studies in Linguistics*, 13 (1958), 1–12. See also Trager's essay in Dell Hymes (ed.), *Language in Culture and Society* (New York, 1964), 274–9.

5 E.g. F. R. Leavis, *English Literature in Our Time and the University* (London, 1969), 149–54.

6 T. S. Eliot, *Selected Essays* (London, 1951), 141–6.

7 See the account of Christopher Ricks's unpublished lecture in *The Times Literary Supplement*, 2 November (1973), 1345. Cf. the subsequent correspondence, 1372, 1404, 1476, 1540 and 1589.

8 Katerina Clark and Michael Holquist, *Mikhail Bakhtin* (Cambridge, Mass., and London, 1985), 10.

9 B. R. McElderry jr., 'Eliot's "Shakespeherian Rag"', *American Quarterly*, 9 (1957), 185–6.

10 Christopher Ricks makes the point that follows, in connection with the same material, in his review of volume VIII of Geoffrey Bullough's *Narrative and Dramatic Sources of Shakespeare* in the *Sunday Times* (London, 9 March 1975).

11 C. F. Tucker Brooke (ed.), *Shakespeare's Plutarch* (London, 1909), 193.

12 For a broader development of these arguments in a different context see my *Shakespeare's Talking Animals* (London, 1973), 15–23 and 178–91.

13 Quoted by Herbert Read in Allen Tate (ed.), *T. S. Eliot: the Man and His Work* (London, 1967), 15.

14 See Harold Jenkins, 'Playhouse Interpolations in the Folio Text of *Hamlet*', *Studies in Bibliography*, XIII (1960), 31–47.

15 Cf. Jenkins, op. cit.: 'An editor who thought so might have a pretty problem on his hands', 42–3.

16 Claude Lévi-Strauss, 'Overture to *Le Cru et le Cuit*', trans. Joseph H. McMahon, in Jacques Ehrmann (ed.), *Structuralism* (New York, 1970), 31–55.

17 ibid., 45.

18 Roland Barthes, *The Pleasure of the Text*, trans. Richard Miller (London, 1976), 9 ff. See also Barthes's essays 'The Third Meaning' and 'The Grain of the Voice' in his *Image-Music-Text*, trans. Stephen Heath (London, 1977), 52–68 and 179–89.

19 Barthes, *The Pleasure of the Text*, 66–7.

20 Eliot, op. cit., 458.

21 Cit. I. A. Richards, *Coleridge on Imagination* (London, 1934; 3rd edn 1962), 84.

5

Telmah

Looking backwards

It begins without words. A man walks out on to the stage and takes up his position, evidently as a sentry. Another man, also evidently a sentry, follows shortly after him. Approaching the first man, the second suddenly halts, seemingly apprehensive and afraid. He quickly raises the long military spear he carries, the partisan, and brings it into an offensive position. That movement – before a word is spoken – immediately pushes the action forward: it enters a different dimension. A mystery has been posited (why are the sentries nervous, why do they make elementary mistakes of military discipline?) and a story starts to unfold.

It ends without words. Two dead bodies are taken up. A troop of soldiers, among them four captains, carries them off, ceremonially and to martial music, after which we hear a 'peal of ordnance'. These sounds, music, the cannon, also forward the action. They imply a new, ordered world of correct military discipline and principled yet firm political rule that will now replace a disordered society riven by betrayal and murder.

At the beginning, it is immediately noticeable that the military are not in complete control. Fundamental errors occur. Bernardo's challenge (and the play's first line), 'Who's there?', is uttered, as Francisco immediately points out, correcting him, by the wrong sentry. The password, 'Long live the King', could hardly be less appropriate: we know that a king has recently not lived long, and that another incumbent will soon cease to live.

At the end, similar misconceptions abound. We know, from what we have seen, that the story Horatio proposes to recount to the 'yet unknowing world' –

> So shall you hear
> Of carnal, bloody, and unnatural acts,
> Of accidental judgments, casual slaughters,
> Of deaths put on by cunning and forc'd cause,
> And, in this upshot, purposes mistook
> Fall'n on th'inventors' heads

(V. ii. 385–90)

– fails adequately to reflect what happened. It was not as simple, as like an 'ordinary' revenge play as that. His solemnity – 'All this can I/Truly deliver' – mocks at the subtleties, the innuendoes, the contradictions, the imperfectly realized motives and sources for action that have been exhibited to us. We are hardly surprised when Fortinbras attempts to sum up Hamlet's potential:

> he was likely, had he been put on,
> To have prov'd most royal

(V. ii. 402–3)

– but his account must, surely, wring a tiny gasp of disbelief from us. Nobody, so far as we have seen (and of course Fortinbras has not seen what we have seen), was likely to have proved less royal. Fortinbras's own claim to authority is decisively undermined by this poor judgement which must strike us as fundamentally mis-conceived. The 'friends' to this present ground, the 'liegemen' to this latest Dane (he is of course 'wrong' even in that, being a Norwegian) may well find the future just as bleak as their mis-taken predecessors.

At the beginning, the action is overshadowed by war: by the 'fair and warlike form' (the Ghost) who dominates it even in his absence. There is much talk of preparation for war.

At the end, the warlike form of Fortinbras also hangs over the action in his absence: he finally obtrudes heralded by a 'warlike noise'. Military rule, by a foreigner, is what lies in store for the Danish state. The war promised at the beginning has not taken place, but at the end the results are the same as if it had.

At the beginning a dead king's presence overhangs the action and the nervousness of the sentries evokes it. At the end another dead king's presence overhangs the action, and is evoked by those final cannons, whose sound has been associated with him throughout.

There is even a mirror reflection of phrases. At the beginning, Bernardo comments, 'How now, Horatio? You tremble and look pale' (I. i. 56). At the end, Hamlet's words echo to a larger audience: 'You that look pale and tremble at this chance' (V. ii. 339).

It would be wrong to make too much of 'symmetries' of this sort, and I mention them only because, once recognized, they help, however slightly, to undermine our inherited notion of *Hamlet* as a structure that runs a satisfactorily linear, sequential course from a firmly established and well-defined beginning through a clearly placed and signalled middle to a causally related and logically determined end which, planted in the beginning, develops, or grows out of it.

Like all symmetries, the ones I have pointed to suggest, not linearity, but circularity: a cyclical and recursive movement wholly at odds with the progressive, incremental ordering that our society, dominated perhaps by a pervasive metaphor of the production line, tends to think of as appropriate to art as to everything else.

If we add to this the judgement that the beginning of *Hamlet* also operates, in a quite perplexing sense, as an ending (the spear's movement forces us to look back to events that have already occurred: the Ghost presupposes a complexity of happenings that lead to its current ghostliness), and that the ending in effect constitutes a beginning (the cannons at the end make us look forward to the new order of Fortinbras, as much as back: Fortinbras's future rule is clearly presaged as the play ends), the complexity of the whole business begins to proliferate.

We can even ask, as amateurs in playhouse dynamics, and in respect of the experience of a live audience in the theatre, when does the play *effectively* begin? Is it when the first sentry walks out on to the stage? Or has the play already begun in our mind's eye as we enter the theatre, leave our house, get up on that morning, buy our ticket some days/weeks ago? In our society, in which *Hamlet* finds itself embedded in the ideology in a variety of roles, the play has, for complex social and historical reasons, always already begun. And on to its beginning we have always already imprinted a knowledge of its course of action, and its ending.

And when, then, does it effectively end? When the dialogue stops and when the soldiers carry the bodies off and the music and the explosion of the cannons is heard? Not really, for there follows applause, and then that complex of revisionary ironies, which we group together under the heading of the 'curtain call'.

This is the ultimate Pirandellian moment which any play reaches: the final moment of closure in all senses which, significantly, raises precisely the question of the nature of closing. Of course, it also nominates the one part of the play normally closed to critical discussion: nobody ever talks about it.[1] Yet the question remains crucial. When *does* the play close? When its 'action' stops? But does not that include, at least to some degree, the curtain call (which, of course, the actors rehearse)? For at this point the actors appear before us only partly as their 'real' selves. They also remain partly, and significantly, still 'in character', retaining mannerisms, perhaps, of the personages they have been playing. Who are they, then, at this point? Hamlet is not the Prince (for he is dead), but he is certainly not the actor who played the Prince either. He does not laugh or caper about as a man might who has scored (in the soccer fashion) a success. He may smile, wanly, as befits one recently slain; he may take, ruefully, the hand of his no less 'dead' opponent Claudius; he may even embrace the long-dead Ophelia. Is not this still acting? (The actor 'playing' himself-as-actor.) Is not this part of the action? It is the part that our applause, that non-discursive aural kind of closure, creates for us. This represents the point at which we assume control, for can we not now make Hamlet go or stay for a longer or shorter time, make him smile, frown, even laugh? It is the point, in short, at which we see the 'edge' of the play before it disappears entirely.

The modern curtain call functions of course very firmly as part of the planned production, fully rehearsed in all its complicated entrances and exits. This in itself gives us a sense of the force of the modern director's feeling that he must *seal* finally and inescapably the 'interpretation' he has thrust on and through the play. Yet the curtain call cannot be thus simply nailed down any more than the play can be thus simply sealed up and made subject to the director's will, however hard he tries. In a way that makes it representative of the play at large, the curtain call slips from under the director's fingers to generate its own wider and wilder implications. Here the play's dead acquire a kind of life once more. Here, most significantly, any apparent movement of the play in one direction halts, and it begins to roll decisively in the opposite direction (if only towards the next performance, when its 'beginning' will emerge again from these smiling actors). In short, the sense of straight, purposive, linear motion forward through the play – the sense required by most 'interpretations' of it – evaporates at the moment of the curtain call, and we sense an opposing current.

In so far as that current connects decisively with elements or aspects of the play already noticed, and in so far as its force seeks to roll the play backwards, reinforcing its recursive mode, making it, as it were, move only unwillingly and haltingly forward, constantly, even as it does so, looking over its own shoulder, then I propose to recognize it and for the sake of convenience and argument to name it in relation to *Hamlet*. I call it *Telmah*: *Hamlet* backwards.

In search of *Telmah*, we can begin by noticing the extent to which looking backwards, re-vision, or re-interpretation, the running of events over again out of their time-sequence, ranks, in effect, as a fundamental aspect of *Hamlet*. Subsequence, posteriority, these are the substantive modes of the opening, generating phrases like 'has this thing appear'd *again* tonight', 'this dreaded sight *twice seen of us*', 'What we have *two nights* seen', 'Thus *twice before*, and jump at this dead hour, . . . hath he gone by our watch' and so on, which eventually provoke the great retailing of past events offered by Horatio as preface to the Ghost's second appearance:

> our last King,
> Whose image even but now appear'd to us,
> Was as you know by Fortinbras of Norway,
> Thereto prick'd on by a most emulate pride,
> Dar'd to the combat; in which our valiant Hamlet
> . . .
> Did slay this Fortinbras, who by a seal'd compact
> Well ratified by law and heraldry
> Did forfeit, with his life, all those his lands
> Which he stood seiz'd of . . .

(I. i. 83–92)

This leads to the full story of Young Fortinbras and so by back-
ward-looking implication brings in, from behind, Hamlet:

> Now, sir, young Fortinbras,
> Of unimprovèd mettle, hot and full,
> Hath in the skirts of Norway here and there
> Shark'd up a list of lawless resolutes
> For food and diet to some enterprise
> That hath a stomach in't, which is no other,
> As it doth well appear unto our state,
> But to recover of us by strong hand
> And terms compulsatory those foresaid lands
> So by his father lost. And this, I take it,
> Is the main motive of our preparations,
> The source of this our watch, and the chief head
> Of this post-haste and rummage in the land.
>
> (I. i. 98–110)

Then, as a sort of climax of this revising, we find Claudius's great
revisionary proposal, his reinterpretation of the past which leads
up to his own present position:

> Though yet of Hamlet our dear brother's death
> The memory be green, and that it us befitted
> To bear our hearts in grief, and our whole kingdom
> To be contracted in one brow of woe,
> Yet so far hath discretion fought with nature
> That we with wisest sorrow think on him
> Together with remembrance of ourselves.
> Therefore our sometime sister, now our queen,
> Th'imperial jointress to this warlike state,
> Have we, as 'twere with a defeated joy,
> With an auspicious and a dropping eye,
> With mirth in funeral and with dirge in marriage,
> In equal scale weighing delight and dole,
> Taken to wife. Nor have we herein barr'd
> Your better wisdoms, which have freely gone
> With this affair along. For all, our thanks.
> Now follows that you know young Fortinbras,
> Holding a weak supposal of our worth . . .
>
> (I. ii. 1–18)

Throughout, it seems to me, the audience of *Hamlet* might legitimately feel that it is being buttonholed, cajoled, persuaded by
participants in the play to look back, to 'revise', to see things
again in particular ways, to 'read' or interpret them along specific
lines and to the exclusion of others. It is a procedure notoriously
mocked by Hamlet himself at the expense of Polonius in a
famously deconstructive moment:

Hamlet: Do you see yonder cloud that's almost in shape of a
camel?
Polonius: By th' mass and 'tis – like a camel indeed.
Hamlet: Methinks it is like a weasel.
Polonius: It is backed like a weasel.
Hamlet: Or like a whale.
Polonius: Very like a whale.

(III. ii. 366–73)

– and easily its most memorable manifestation occurs when the
Ghost buttonholes the Prince with a peculiarly insistent version
of the murder:

Brief let me be. Sleeping within my orchard,
My custom always of the afternoon,
Upon my secure hour thy uncle stole
With juice of cursed hebenon in a vial,
And in the porches of my ears did pour
The leperous distilment, whose effect
Holds such an enmity with blood of man
That swift as quicksilver it courses through
The natural gates and alleys of the body,
And with a sudden vigour it doth posset
And curd, like eager droppings into milk,
The thin and wholesome blood. So did it mine,
And a most instant tetter bark'd about,
Most lazar-like, with vile and loathsome crust
All my smooth body.

(I. v. 59–73)

These slow-motion 'action replays' of past events become a
feature of the play. It seems constantly to 'revise' itself in this
way and this serves to pull back against any 'forward' progressive movement which it might otherwise appear to instigate.

On a larger scale, a series of insistent thematic rhythms seems to run counter to or – better word – syncopate with those apparently fostered by the play's sequential development. The death of fathers, which Claudius stresses as a 'common theme' – one which has reason's backing in his assertion 'this must be so'

> But you must know your father lost a father,
> That father lost, lost his
>
> (I. ii. 89–90)

– nevertheless begins to bulk disconcertingly large. It is almost a case of paternal overkill. By the middle of the play our attention has been forcefully drawn to the death of no fewer than *five* fathers: King Fortinbras; King Hamlet; Polonius; Priam; and Gonzago, the Player King. In three of the cases an avenging son presents himself: Fortinbras; Hamlet; Laertes. The pattern seems to push Hamlet, in his role as revenger, into the foreground. But then we notice the countervailing pattern hinted at by and available within the same structure: that which focuses on the dead father's brother, who, as *uncle* to the son, controls and redirects the son's revenging energies. The clearest case involves Young Fortinbras, whose uncle Norway has succeeded to the throne, whereupon he reintegrates the displaced Young Fortinbras into the society. This rhythm is underscored when Claudius tries to perform exactly the same operation in respect of Hamlet: as uncle who has taken over the throne, he tries famously to reintegrate the displaced Hamlet into the society. And it is underscored again when, the operation having failed with Hamlet, Claudius assumes the avuncular role in respect of Laertes after Polonius's death and, again famously, redirects his revenging energy and integrates him into the society. In short, the death of all these fathers serves to establish and to sound a counter-balancing 'avuncular' chord that reverberates deep within the play's harmonic structure.

The avuncular function seen in opposition to the paternal one then becomes a palpable aspect of the range of themes *Hamlet* deploys. The opposition derives from and works consistently with traditional European conceptualizations which construct the father as a figure of stern discipline and authority, and the uncle as a contrary figure of laxity and good humour. Claudius notoriously abrogates this disposition of polarities (Hamlet's

99

bitter description of him as 'my uncle–father' reinforces the collapse of meaningful categories) and thus commits a transgression as destructive as the one collaterally perpetrated by Gertrude. For European culture permits the transformation wife–mother, but forbids, or is deeply suspicious of the transformation mother–wife, since that raises the spectre of incest.[2] In becoming an 'aunt–mother' and so a wife, Gertrude, like Claudius, violates fundamental distinctions and undermines their use as instruments for the generation of meaning.

The insistent, nagging quality of these aspects of the play acts as an apparently 'disruptive' element in *Hamlet* because it finally serves to promote Claudius. Its 'catchy' pulse wins the attention, and draws it away from the Prince. Claudius ceases to be the simple stage-villain described by the Ghost and required by the smoothing-over process of interpretation that linear progression demands. He has many more than one role, and these are intricate and manifold. He functions as brother (even the primal brother, Cain, as he himself suggests), father, in a legal and political sense to Hamlet, lover and later husband to Gertrude, murderer of King Hamlet, monarch, and political head of state. In a sense, all these roles congregate within his enormously forceful role of uncle on the basis of which his opposition to Hamlet is determined. He becomes, as the play terms him, no simple villain, but a complex, compelling figure, Hamlet's 'mighty opposite', whose mightiness constantly tugs back, recursively, against the smooth flow of a play that bears, perhaps surprisingly, only the Prince's name. It is not insignificant that, at the play's most recursive moment, in the performance of another play, the murderer (Lucianus) is clearly and coolly presented as a nephew, murdering his uncle. In this play-within-the-play, right at the centre of *Hamlet*, *Telmah* disconcertingly surfaces.

The Mousetrap marks *Hamlet*'s most recursive moment: the point at which time runs most obviously backwards, and where the play does not just glance over its shoulder, so much as turn fully round to look squarely at the most prominent action replay of them all. More than a play-within-a-play, *The Mousetrap* offers a replay of a replay: the Ghost's revisionary account of the murder, fitted out with actions. Equally, in so far as the design of *The Mousetrap* aims decisively to generate events that will forward the action of *Hamlet*, it also firmly looks towards the future. It functions, as Hamlet himself says, 'tropically': that is, as both trope or metaphor, and as the 'tropic' or turning point of the play. For *Hamlet* to operate, the past has here to be causally fused to what lies ahead: *Hamlet*'s linear progression depends on that, and the Prince himself has made it a condition of his own future actions. The Ghost's account of the events leading up to King Hamlet's murder are here to be tested by means of asking an audience at the play to read them in a particular way.

Hamlet himself is confident: he has written part of the play and proves 'as good as a chorus' in interpreting it. Rarely can someone involved in a drama have been so convinced that, in its linear, sequential unfolding, its single, unequivocal meaning will receive ready, interpreted acknowledgement. Like the play which bears his name, the Prince seems committed, purposive, moving inexorably to a predetermined end. Like *Hamlet*, confirming its enclosing presence perhaps, the play-within-the-play begins without words. And then, suddenly, it all goes wrong. *The Mousetrap* becomes 'tropical' indeed. *Hamlet* 'turns' decisively. It turns into *Telmah*.

To the Sunderland station

The scene now shifts to a train proceeding from Leeds to Sunderland one Saturday evening in November 1917.

On that train, a man is opening his mail. Amongst his letters he finds a square envelope containing the issue of the *Modern Language Review* (XII, 4) for October 1917. Leafing through it, he finds himself attracted to a particular article and 'all unconscious of impending fate', as he puts it, begins to read.

The effect, to say the least, is odd. In fact, he later uses the term 'overwhelming' and speaks of the experience as capable of throwing 'any mind off its balance'. The man was the scholar and critic John Dover Wilson, then aged 36. The article was by W. W. Greg and it was entitled 'Hamlet's Hallucination'.

The thrust of Greg's article lies in his clear perception that something goes badly wrong with the Prince's plans right at the beginning of *The Mousetrap*. Claudius fails to make any response to that initial and vital 'action replay', the dumb-show. The 'full significance' of this, Greg argues, has never been appreciated. After all, the dumb-show presents the stark details of Claudius's supposed crime, in more or less exactly the form retailed by the Ghost. Claudius's failure to respond means, quite simply, that the Ghost has failed the test, organized by Hamlet himself, to establish its veracity.

There is no doubt, of course, that Claudius has murdered King Hamlet. The doubts are as to the mode and method of the act – and in this respect the Ghost is clearly revealed, Greg says, to fall short as an 'objective' reporter. He has not given Hamlet true information. The 'orthodox view' of the play, which requires an objective truth-bearing Ghost, with Claudius properly indicted by its testimony as the dastardly poisoning villain of the story, ignores or tries to think 'around' the dumb-show. It argues, say, that the King and Queen are in close conversation at the time and so pay no attention to what is going on. This explanation, says Greg, 'is indeed a lame one': it treats the play as 'history' not drama. Such critics enquire 'why Hamlet behaved in a ridiculous way, when the question they should have asked was why Shakespeare did – or whether he did'. He adds, remarkably for 1917, 'this tendency is particularly prominent in the work of A. C. Bradley'.

For Greg, the 'extraordinary nature' of the dumb-show needs to be grasped. If we do so, we can see how genuinely upsetting Claudius's negative response to it is. Its effect is to advance or 'upgrade' Claudius: to make him more intriguing, his actions and his motives more complex: to make him a *victim* of the Ghost's malicious reportage as much as a villain in terms of the way the play is usually seen: to confirm him, in the play's terms, as no simple moustache-twirling criminal, but Hamlet's 'mighty opposite'; an impressive figure of potentially tragic stature who calls for a degree of sympathetic attention that must inevitably pull against the response traditionally inspired by the Prince. For an orthodox Hamlet-centred interpretation of the play, Claudius's negative reaction to the dumb-show 'not merely threatens the logical structure of one of the most crucial scenes of the play, but reduces it to meaningless confusion'. As a result, Greg concludes, 'we have to choose between giving up Shakespeare as a rational playwright, and giving up our inherited beliefs regarding the story of *Hamlet*'.

Nearly seventy years later, something of the panache of Greg's argument still communicates itself to us, though its potential as light reading for a Yorkshire Saturday night and Sunday morning might perhaps be a matter for dispute. What cannot be disputed is its effect on Dover Wilson. I have described this as odd: a better phrase might be 'seriously disturbing', even 'mind-blowing'. He himself describes it as 'an intensely felt experience' which resulted in 'a state of some considerable excitement'. It filled him, he reports, with 'a sort of insanity', and cast upon him, in his own words of eighteen years later, 'a spell which changed the whole tenor of my existence, and still dominates it in part'. Give up Shakespeare as a rational playwright indeed! Give up our inherited beliefs! Having read the article 'half a dozen times before reaching Sunderland' an almost Pauline sense of mission seems to have descended upon him: 'from the first [I] realized that I had been born to answer it'.

Why such a heated response to an article in a learned journal? And why – perhaps more interestingly – is it recorded in such detail eighteen years later, as part of the prolegomena to Dover Wilson's *What Happens in Hamlet* (1935)? We might, of course, pick up the not-quite-covert hint that the response is itself engagingly Hamlet-like. Dover Wilson describes what he calls his own 'spiritual condition' at the time as 'critical, not to say dangerous, a condition in which a man becomes converted, falls in love, or gives way to a mania for wild speculation'. The war had its pressures, we are given to understand, and it perhaps did not seem inappropriate – it might even seem appealing – that a personality so highly charged might experience a reaction to such a situation which could be, as another critic was to put it of Hamlet, 'in excess of the facts as they appear'.

Of course, a lot depends on how the facts are made to appear. And just as a rather different *Hamlet* – *Telmah* – can be detected struggling beneath – or with – that play, so a rather different explanation of Dover Wilson's response may be heard rustling uneasily on the edge of any half-hint of the Prince-like nature of its author's entirely winsome 'insanity'.

We can begin with the fact that, in November 1917, the war was not the only source of deep-seated disturbance in the world. In fact we could point out that, on any of the Saturdays in that month, news of the impending or actual Bolshevik revolution in Russia was likely to have been competing with news from the fronts. We have Dover Wilson's own statement that 'I found it difficult to concentrate upon anything unconnected with the War' and even his comment that, spending a lot of his time in trains, 'the hours of travel were mostly occupied in reading the newspapers'.

A glance at the newspapers of November 1917 confirms that the Bolshevik action received wide coverage, and one could reasonably assume Dover Wilson's awareness of the events from that. On Saturday 3 November, *The Times* reported 'Persistent rumours in Petrograd of the imminence of armed action by the Maximalists [i.e. Bolsheviks] whose object is to seize the supreme power' (p. 6). The *coup* actually took place on Wednesday/Thursday, 7–8 November (by the Russian calendar this was October 25/26). On Friday 9 November, extensive reports appeared in *The Times*: 'Anarchy in Petrograd: Power Seized by Lenin' with editorial comment of a predictable nature: 'the most extreme party in the Soviet appears to be in power . . . it is assuredly not the authentic voice of Russia'. By Saturday 10 November, what *The Times* was then calling 'The Lenin Revolution' was fully reported, together with an extensive account of what the headlines termed the 'Siege of the Winter Palace', and on both Saturday 17 November and Saturday 24 November there appeared lengthy reports headed 'Civil Strife in Petrograd' and 'Russia's Starving Armies', etc. It would have been difficult in fact for a newspaper reader to be unaware of these events.

However, it adds a dimension to the picture, and gives something of an edge to what we may presume to be the *quality* of Dover Wilson's awareness, if we take into account the nature of the mission on which he was currently engaged: his reason, that is, for being on that particular train at that particular time.

Dover Wilson's main employment then was as a school inspector of the Board of Education, stationed at Leeds. But, in common with other inspectors, he was also from time to time used in some war work: specifically, as an inspector for the Ministry of Munitions. The reason why he was travelling to Sunderland had to do with that work, and with a particular crisis concerning it. 'Some trouble', as he decorously puts it, 'had arisen with local trade-union officials' in Sunderland, and Dover Wilson had been urgently dispatched there to sort it out.

It is worth very briefly reminding ourselves that the Ministry of Munitions presented at that time an unusual and, to some, a rather dangerous spectacle in terms of British labour relations. The pressures of the war (including the arrival of women workers) had created a situation in which, to use A. J. P. Taylor's words, the local shop stewards 'were often revolutionary socialists . . . some of them were opposed to the war'. This meant that they found themselves frequently in conflict with 'official' and conservative trade union policy, since they represented a much wider working-class interest in the face of it. Ministers such as Lloyd George and, by 1917, Churchill were forced to work 'hand in hand with the revolutionary shop stewards' despite 'growls of protest' from the unions.[3]

For 'trouble' to occur at any time in the munitions industry was obviously bad enough. Negotiations at local level with what were later indeed called 'Bolshevik' shop stewards[4] must have been, if you will pardon the expression, a potentially explosive business. Such trouble occurring in November 1917 would certainly have had a capacity for uncontrolled detonation more than sufficient to generate a 'critical, not to say dangerous' condition (we should note Dover Wilson's submerged metaphor of impending combustion) in a man about to be ignited by a copy of the *Modern Language Review*.

Insurrection was in the air. On the first day of the Bolshevik *coup* (7 November), speaking, by chance, in the House of Lords, the Marquess of Salisbury had warned that 'The governing classes hitherto had been inclined to regard the working class as a sort of dangerous animal of enormous strength and great potential violence, which it was necessary to be very civil to, but never to trust' (*The Times*, 8 November 1917, p. 12). In short, the revolutionary proposals of Greg's article on *Hamlet* must have fallen into a powder keg of a mind already in some degree prepared to be 'blown' into 'a sort of insanity' by them just as, in the wider context towards which the Leeds–Sunderland train seemed to be speeding, certain events were already shaking the world.

Before dismissing this view as one which makes far too much of a mere coincidence of dates, certain other aspects of what is really rather a complex situation should be borne in mind. First, it is Dover Wilson himself who gives all the facts, as it were compulsively, in a 'letter' entitled 'The Road to Elsinore, being an Epistle Dedicatory to Walter Wilson Greg' which prefaces his major and highly influential book *What Happens in Hamlet* (1935).

The apparently immodest, unreserved commitment to total exposition of that book's title lends its own confessional, bean-spilling air to the letter, and *vice versa*.

The literary device of the publicly printed letter has always, of course, exploited means of communication generated by its paradoxical mode. As a document whose standing is both private and public at the same time, it 'means' both by what it is seen to offer, in confidence, and by what it is seen to withhold, in public. It operates, that is to say, both directly, by intimate revelation, and indirectly by evident obfuscation and suppression. The two methods of signifying are equated and intimately involved. What such a letter says and what it does not say, its utterances and its silences, are both meaningful: each becomes an aspect of the other. In *this* letter, the overt commitment is to the whole truth. Greg is told, 'you may have guessed something of this, but you cannot know it all'. The letter will thus tell all. It will explain 'the origin and purpose of this book', take us to the final originary source of what happened before *What Happens in Hamlet* happened, and thus lead us, in effect, to the root cause of its writing. That origin is precisely, specifically and insistently dated in a spirit of 'classic realism': 'It begins some time in the November of 1917. . . . I reached home one Saturday evening to find an urgent telephone message awaiting me.' The related, concomitant silence, however, is no less insistent. There is absolutely no mention before or after of the Bolshevik revolution.

I think we can regard that silence as resonant, and not simply because of the interest of the revolution itself, or because of any potential connection, however oblique, between it and Dover Wilson's current journey (Sunderland lacks a Winter Palace, but things have to start somewhere). It could be seen finally as a matter of discourse. The discourse of literary criticism in Britain and America, then and now, tends to exclude the area of politics as not overtly appropriate to itself and its purposes. It would seem literally unreasonable for a literary critic to take such issues on board as, no doubt, it seems unreasonable for me to do so right now.

But in fact, the truth is that Dover Wilson had to hand, and was perfectly capable of using, another discourse designed exactly for that purpose. There is, it seems to me, great significance in respect of the way discourses operate in the fact that he makes no mention of the Bolshevik revolution. For it means that no mention is made of it, no connection drawn between it and his present highly emotional state on the part of a man who had lived within the Russian Empire (in Finland) for three years, who by his own account had become, on his return to Britain, 'a well known public lecturer' on the subject of Russia, who was currently, as he writes to Greg, making 'fitful and unsuccessful attempts to learn Russian' and who on more than one previous occasion had written coolly, seriously, and at length about exactly this possibility of revolution in Russia and its likely consequences.

In 1906, Dover Wilson's article 'The Aims and Methods of the Social Revolutionary Party in Russia' appeared in the *Independent Review* (XI, pp. 137–50). It begins by making my central point for me: that a revolution in Russia (he is referring of course to the revolution of 1905) must be an event of considerable significance for Western Europe and that there can be no excuse for any suppression of awareness of it:

> The newspapers have been undeniably generous in the space devoted to the 'Russian Revolution', and no Englishman has any excuse for being ignorant of the fact that, from one end to the other of the great eastern plain of Europe which we agree to call Russia, a gigantic civil war is now being waged – a war which must to a large extent determine the destinies not only of Russia, but also of Europe as a whole.

The piece goes on to make what, even to my entirely unsophisticated eyes, appears as a somewhat over-simple analysis of Russia's political structure. 'Russia possesses only two revolutionary factions of any real importance: the Social Revolutionaries and the Social Democrats.' But naive or not, the future reader of Greg's revolutionary proposals concerning *Hamlet* leaves us in no doubt that of those factions, the programme of the Social Revolutionaries is infinitely preferable to that advanced by the Social Democrats. The latter, being 'founded on the theories of a German doctrinaire', can have no success in the face of the former, whose Fabian mode especially recommends it and ensures, for Dover Wilson, that it finds its basis in 'real Russian institutions'. The future of the country thus 'clearly lies with the Social Revolutionaries', a situation confirmed by the fact that the wretched Social Democrats had recently split into two parties, the Minority and the Majority, thus demonstrating their hopelessness. These two factions could confidently be consigned to outer darkness and forgotten. The Social Revolutionaries, whose policy of terrorism Dover Wilson explains, condones and approves (he says it seems to be having 'a distinctly beneficial result'), win his support, for 'the future of the country lies with them'.

Everybody makes mistakes, and a man who has espoused the cause of the Social Revolutionary party so wholeheartedly – even to the extent of condoning its commitment to terrorism – and who has so roundly dismissed the claims of the competing Social Democrats, whether Menshevik (as the Minority group was called) or Bolshevik (as the Majority group was called), a man who has uttered so confidently might reasonably and significantly fall silent on the subject.

In fact, Dover Wilson committed himself yet again to the same issue in 1914. Writing a piece called 'Russia and her Ideals' in the *Round Table* for December of that year (V, 17, pp. 103–35), he offers, in his own words, to correct prejudices: to look Russia 'straight in the eyes, that we may hope to catch a glimpse of her soul'. The glimpse reveals, he assures us, a deep craving for order, arising out of a constant struggle for self-preservation. Autocracy comes almost naturally to be the only form of government for such a society: 'A State whose very existence is perpetually at stake, for whom discipline is the primary need, has really no choice but to place itself in the hands of an imperator, a Caesar, a Tsar.' As a result, autocracy in Russia is best seen as 'part of religion itself', with the Tsar as God's 'representative upon earth'. Anything more complex, he concludes, would only puzzle the Russians, for Tsardom is more than autocracy in their case; it is theocracy. And he adds, with the confidence of one who has gazed 'straight in the eyes' of the 'teeming millions', 'As both it is intensely representative of the national mind and character'.

The principle of autocracy, he continues, is thus the only principle that mind and that character can understand, and it would therefore be wrong to countenance any disturbance of it. Autocracy, he assures us – in 1914 –

still has a long life before it and much work to perform in Russia. It is therefore wiser to face the facts and to recognize

that the Tsardom is after all Russia's form of democracy . . . it is
the kind of government the people understand and reverence,
and it is their only protection against the tyranny of an aristo-
cratic clique . . . when the will of the autocrat is clearly and
unmistakably expressed, it has always been found to corre-
spond with the needs of the people. . . . The picture of Russia as
a land of domestic tyranny and unhappiness is altogether false.

Those who asked, 'How wrong can you be?' of Dover Wilson's
1906 article are partly answered here. You can be *much* wronger.
But the piece is certainly not without interest on another level.
World-picture fanciers will already have recognized in it a
version of what, by the time of the Second World War, had
become a standard British response to national crisis: the construction of long-past, green, alternative worlds of percipient
peasants, organic communities, festivals, folk-art, and absolute
monarchy to set against present chaos. Dover Wilson's revised
Russian world picture of 1914 has developed, since his essay of
1906, features which surface regularly in our century as part of a
recurrent siege mentality. It thus has much more than a coinci-
dental resemblance to E. M. W. Tillyard's well-known war effort,
The Elizabethan World Picture of 1943. A discourse which, seeking
for the final, confirming presence of authority, nominates the
linchpin of the political structure as 'God's representative on
earth' is clearly heard in both.[5] Each represents, less an accurate
picture of the world it purports to describe, than an intimate,
covert measure of its author's fears about the fallen world in
which he currently lives, and in the face of which he has constructed a peculiarly English Eden.

But it is not just a question of getting it wrong, wronger, or
wrongest. The point is that the decided modification in Dover
Wilson's views about Russia which takes place between 1906 and
1914, moving from an early commitment to Fabianism to a subsequent rejection of that in favour of Tsarism, represents a
serious narrowing of options, a growing sense of urgency, and a
harder and harder line. And it is thus a modification which, given
the previous confidence about insights into 'national mind and
character', must have lent the *actual* events of November 1917,
when they occurred, the quality of a nightmare; turning them
into a horror of such proportions that perhaps no overt response

to them was possible. (His later embarrassment over his writings on Russia is evident in his autobiography: 'I could not prophesy', he admits, 'a portent like Lenin who arrived in 1917.')

This is what I mean when I say that the absence of any mention of the Bolshevik revolution in Dover Wilson's account of his train journey strikes me as significant. It signifies of course that the Bolshevik revolution *is* in effect being responded to, coped with, in that 'intensely felt experience', that 'spell which changed the whole tenor of my existence', and that 'sort of insanity' provoked by Greg's article on *Hamlet*.

Greg's attack, after all, is on the smooth surface of the play, seen as the product of Shakespeare the 'rational playwright', but effectively, of course, created by an 'orthodox' interpretation which seeks for unity, progression, coherence and, if possible, sequential ordering in all art, as part of a ruthless and rigorous process of domestication. There is no obvious way of placating Greg's objections to that sort of *Hamlet* for they constitute a frontal assault on what he terms the 'inherited beliefs' – that brand of literary Tsarism – which reinforce and sustain it. And the assault is certainly not Fabian in character. It is directly, violently Bolshevik.

Dover Wilson's defence took various forms. There was an immediate diagnostic response to the editor of the *Modern Language Review* by means of a postcard dispatched upon alighting from the train at Sunderland, which went so far as to nominate Greg as an unwitting agent of the arch-revolutionary himself: 'Greg's article devilish ingenious but damnably wrong', it twinkled, and offered a rejoinder, which duly appeared. There followed two major salvoes: the edition of *Hamlet* prepared by Dover Wilson for the New Cambridge Shakespeare in 1934 – a series of which, provoked into the role by Greg's article, he says, he had become general editor in 1919 – and the book *What Happens in Hamlet*, which purports to release him from thrall to the problems, by telling all. Those interested in the details of his argument can pursue them there. Suffice it to say that I do not myself find them convincing, so much as replete with the charm and ingenuity of the truly desperate. To suggest that Claudius does not notice the dumb-show, engaged as he is in conversation with Polonius and Gertrude, seeks to 'naturalize' the situation out of existence. The further suggestion that the Players (a

burlesque of Edward Alleyn and Shakespeare's rivals the Lord
Admiral's Men) constitute a kind of surly trade union, engaged in
a dispute with their temporary boss, Hamlet, which provokes an
unlooked-for work-to-rule, resulting in an unauthorized dumb-
show as embarrassing to Hamlet as it is ineffective in respect of
Claudius, so nearly proves my own point for me that I hesitate to
use it, although connoisseurs will find it on pp. 153–63 of *What
Happens in Hamlet*.

But if these salvoes represent Dover Wilson's defence against
Bolshevism in its specifically displaced Shakespearian form, it is
possible also to suggest that the same battle was subsequently
taken up on a broader front by the same combatant. Two years
later, in May 1919, a departmental committee was appointed by
the president of the Board of Education to investigate what was
termed 'The Teaching of English in England'. Its terms of reference were

> To inquire into the position occupied by English (Language and
> Literature) in the educational system of England, and to advise
> how its study may best be promoted in schools of all types,
> including Continuation Schools, and in Universities and other
> Institutions of Higher Education, regard being had to
>
> (1) the requirements of a liberal education;
> (2) the needs of business, the professions, and public services;
>   and
> (3) the relation of English to other studies.

The committee's chairman was Sir Henry Newbolt, and prominent amongst its members was John Dover Wilson.

Many things have been said about the Newbolt Report, as the
published findings of the committee became known. The first
thing to stress is that it was widely influential. It sold, in Dover
Wilson's words, 'like a best-seller', and it can be said effectively
to have shaped the nature of 'English' as the academic subject we
know today. Its spiritual father is Matthew Arnold, its spiritual
son F. R. Leavis. Its two central concerns – more or less overt –
are related political ones: social cohesion in the face of potential
disintegration and disaffection; and nationalism, the encourage-
ment of pride in English national culture on a broader front. The
common coin of its discourse is generated by concepts we have

already encountered: notably those of 'national mind and character'. English, seen in this light, becomes 'the only basis possible
for national education', being not merely the medium of our
thought, but 'the very stuff and process of it. It is itself the English
mind.' An education based on English would thus have a 'unify-
ing tendency', acting as an antidote to the divisiveness, the
'bitterness and disintegration' of a class-dominated society. It
would heal one of the major causes of 'division amongst us': the
'undue narrowness of the ground on which we meet for the true
purposes of social life' (without specifying what those might be).
Recognizing that we are 'not one nation but two', the report sees
the study of English as capable of bridging, if not closing, the
'chasm of separation', the 'mental [sic] distances between
classes'. Offering a 'bond of union between classes' it would
'beget the right kind of national pride'.[6]

The committee was in effect responding to the sort of view
promoted, oddly enough, by the Welshman Lloyd George, when
the war ended. Speaking at Manchester in September 1918, he
had put the case that

> The most formidable institution we had to fight in Germany
> was not the arsenals of Krupps or the yards in which they
> turned out submarines, but the schools of Germany. They were
> our most formidable competitors in business and our most
> terrible opponents in war. An educated man is a better worker,
> a more formidable warrior, and a better citizen.[7]

The Education Acts of 1918 (the Fisher Act) and 1944 (the Butler
Act) are testimony to the fact that in Britain the threat of external
disruption usually acts as the parent of educational change.
Certainly by 1919 events outside the United Kingdom had
evidently carried a clear enough message to ministers within it. If
there was a breathless hush in the close of Europe, it was not
inappropriate that a committee chaired by Sir Henry Newbolt
(for it is he) should be urging us, through the study of English
language and literature, to 'play up, play up, and play the game'.

Members of the committee were allotted areas of special
concern and amongst those assigned to Dover Wilson, he later
tells us, was the one which appears in the report as Sections
232–8, 'Literature and the Nation'. The thrust of these pages
(252–60) argues that teaching literature to the working class is a

kind of 'missionary work' aimed at stemming the tide of that class's by then evident disaffection. The missionary to Sunderland clearly sees that workers need to be embraced into the larger way of British life, and he leaves us in no doubt that this is a matter 'involving grave national issues' to which the committee has given 'much anxious thought' (p. 252).

Workers, such 'thought' urges, ought to feel that a national culture exists to which they can belong, and literature is offered as an instrument for promoting social cohesion in its name. Its political role is quite clear:

> Literature, in fact, seems to be classed by a large number of thinking working men with antimacassars, fish-knives and other unintelligible and futile trivialities of 'middle-class culture', and, as a subject of instruction, is suspect as an attempt 'to side-track the working-class movement'. We regard the prevalence of such opinions as a serious matter, not merely because it means the alienation of an important section of the population from the 'confort' and 'mirthe' of literature, but chiefly because it points to a morbid condition of the body politic which if not taken in hand may be followed by lamentable consequences. For if literature be, as we believe, an embodiment of the best thoughts of the best minds, the most direct and lasting communication of experience by man to men, a fellowship which 'binds together by passion and knowledge the vast empire of human society, as it is spread over the whole earth, and over all time', then the nation of which a considerable portion rejects this means of grace, and despises this great spiritual influence, must assuredly be heading to disaster.[8]

As another member of the committee put it, 'Deny to working class children any common share in the immaterial and presently they will grow into the men who demand with menaces a communism of the material.'[9]

The spectre of a working class demanding material goods with menaces, losing its national mind, besmirching its national character, clearly had a growing capacity to disturb after the events of 1917, particularly if that class, as Dover Wilson writes in the Newbolt Report, sees education 'mainly as something to equip them to fight their capitalistic enemies. In the words of one young worker "Yes, what you say is all right – but will that sort of stuff bring us more bread and cheese?" ' (ibid.). To Dover Wilson – and to many others subsequently – the solution lay quite clearly in the sort of nourishment that English literature offered: the snap, crackle and pop of its roughage, a purgative force of considerable political power – not because it has a direct influence on what Dover Wilson (and others) called 'the social problem', but because of its indirect influence on what they certainly did not call ideology, but which is clearly signalled as such in the report's references to a general, indeed a national, 'state of mind'. If the 'state of mind' is orientated wholly towards the 'social problem', the result is an unhealthy imbalance:

> This state of mind is not a new thing in history, and even goes back as far as Plato. It finds a parallel in the contempt for 'poets, pipers, players, jesters and such-like caterpillars of the common-wealth' expressed by puritans of the 16th and 17th centuries, and in the hostility towards the 'culture of capitalism' now prevalent in Bolshevist Russia.[10]

That hostility, that Bolshevism, is apparently best met by strengthening the character, through massive doses of poetry administered by a solicitous education system:

> we believe that, if rightly presented, poetry will be recognized by the most ardent social reformers as of value, because while it contributes no specific solution of the social problem it endows the mind with power and sanity; because, in a word, it enriches personality.[11]

Personality! The very word is like a bell. The ideological position this signals – the commitment to individualism as a long-term solution to the social problem – is a familiar one, and it remains the long-term position from which most teaching of literature is still mounted. Its political, economic and social implications are clearly spelled out in the Newbolt Report, and most clearly in those parts of the report which we know were written by Dover Wilson. The impulse generating that position, the stimulus to which it constitutes a considered response, lies in the events which took place in Russia in November 1917, and the subsequent sense of betrayal on the Allies' part in the face of the consequent German spring offensive of 1918 which nearly won the war for the Kaiser.

My point is a simple one. Dover Wilson's response to Greg's article on that train to Sunderland in 1917 offers an excellent example of the sort of interaction between literary interpretation and political and social concerns that always pertains, but normally remains covert in our culture. Confronted by what I have called a manifestation of *Telmah* – i.e. by the disruption of the normally smooth and, in terms of individual 'personality' (Hamlet's or Shakespeare's), explainable surface of a text that our society has appropriated as a manifestation of great (and thus reassuring) art – he replies with a vigour and an emotionally charged nervous energy appropriate to it as what in fact it must have seemed to be: an attack or an offensive mounted against the structure of civilization as we know it – in short, an attack on our ideology. Dover Wilson's sensitivity to overt political attacks – manifested in his articles on revolutionary Russia – fuels his response to *Telmah*, which he rightly senses as potentially revolutionary in ideological terms. Today *Hamlet*, tomorrow the World! We might in passing note, as Dover Wilson himself does, recalling the astonishing output by J. M. Robertson, E. E. Stoll, L. L. Schücking and others in the twelve months of 1919, that 'For some reason or other, the War acted as a stimulus to the study of *Hamlet*.'[12]

As a member of the Newbolt Committee, as we have seen, he insists on the proper, controlled study of literature as essential to a society wishing to avoid the alien barbarities of Bolshevism and to preserve the 'national mind and character', i.e. the integral and coherent structures of a British way of life. Years later, writing on the work of the Workers' Educational Association classes, he comments that, but for them 'the abysmal disillusion that followed the end of the First World War . . . might well have resulted in revolution'. *Telmah*'s proposed reversal, its upturning, topsy-turvy mode (in which the Ghosts of one's fathers are not to be trusted), would undoubtedly have come hard to one whose very name invokes the clear, defining boundaries of an established island culture. *Telmah*'s threatened incursion would therefore have to face the determined opposition of those impregnable white cliffs, and the forces assembled – indeed, symbolized – by the figure of Sir Henry Newbolt.

Names, after all, are invested with potency. Dover Wilson's autobiography is in fact entitled *Milestones on the Dover Road* and thus half-humorously hints at his own eponymic standing whilst memorializing his role as defender of the British national mind, character and culture. His article of 1914, in favour of Tsardom, is naturally anonymous. His earlier piece of 1906, with its efforts to bury Bolshevism, nevertheless offers an appealing recognition of the literally topsy-turvy function of revolution which I have tried weakly to hint at in my formulation of the name *Telmah*. Confronting Bolshevism, Dover Wilson unwittingly becomes its Greg. For what does that article do but argue that the spectre haunting Europe certainly cannot be trusted? It would be nice to report that an intimate and deeply personal sense of revolution and reversal accompanied these efforts to heap oblivion on Bolshevism. I can, and do. The article is signed, not John Dover Wilson, but Wildover Johnson.

It would also be nice to conclude by turning back, now, to the play. But in a very serious sense, which I hope to have made clear, we cannot do so. There is no unitary, self-presenting play for us to turn back to, and I have no intention of turning myself inside out like Wildover Johnson in pursuit of a smoothed-over (or smooth Dover) interpretation of it which can then be offered gift-wrapped, as the truth. That kind of 'appeasement' of the text can be said to have its own political analogues. And indeed . . . 'Dear Dr Dover Wilson' begins a missive from Birmingham dated 7 June 1936:

> I expect you will be rather surprised to get a letter from me as we have not been 'introduced'. But as we are both public characters perhaps we may dispense with formalities. . . . I can't help telling you what immense pleasure I have had out of *What Happens in Hamlet*. I had asked for it as a Christmas present, and when it duly appeared I sat up several nights into the small hours reading it. . . . When I had finished it, I did what I don't think I have ever done before with any book: I immediately read it all over again! And that won't be the last time of reading.

The letter was signed 'Neville Chamberlain'.[13]

In short, I am not going to suggest that we can approach *Hamlet* by recognizing *Telmah*, or that *Telmah* is the real play, obscured by *Hamlet*. That would be to try to reconcile, to bring to peace, to appease a text whose vitality resides precisely in its plurality: in the fact that it contradicts itself and strenuously resists our attempts to resolve, to domesticate that contradiction. I am trying to suggest that its contradiction has value in that a pondering of some of the attempts that have been made to resolve it, to make the play speak coherently, within a limited set of boundaries, reveals the political, economic and social forces to which all such 'interpretation' responds and in whose name it must inevitably, if covertly, be made.[14] I am not suggesting an 'alternative' reading of *Hamlet*, because that would be to fall into the same trap. I offer my title of *Telmah* as what it is: a sense of an ever-present potential challenge and contradiction *within* and *implied by* the text that we name *Hamlet*. In this sense, *Telmah* coexists with, is coterminous with, *Hamlet* in a way that must strike us, finally, as impossible. A thing, we are taught, cannot be both what it is and another thing. But that is precisely the principle challenged by *Telmah*. Our notion that it cannot coexist with *Hamlet* marks the limit, I suggest, of our Eurocentric view of 'sense', of 'order', of 'presence' if you like, and of 'point of view'. That Eurocentricity lies behind and validates a limited notion of 'interpretation' which will allow us to have *Hamlet* in various guises, and will also, as an alternative, allow clever and sophisticated interpreters to have, say, *Telmah*. But it will not allow us to have both, because that would explode our notion of the single and unified 'point of view' whose 'authority', as that term suggests, derives from its source, the author.

And yet, to conclude, we only have to step beyond the shores of Europe to encounter quite a different notion of interpretation which will allow exactly what I propose: the sense of a text as a site, or an area of conflicting and often contradictory potential interpretations, no one or group of which can claim 'intrinsic' primacy or 'inherent' authority, and all of which are always ideological in nature and subject to extrinsic political and economic determinants.

The abstract model I reach for is of course that of jazz music: that black American challenge to the Eurocentric idea of the author's, or the composer's, authority. For the jazz musician, the 'text' of a melody is a means, not an end. Interpretation in that context is not parasitic but symbiotic in its relationship with its object. Its role is not limited to the service, or the revelation, or the celebration of the author's/composer's art. Quite the reverse: interpretation *constitutes* the art of the jazz musician. The same unservile principle seems to me to be appropriate to the critic's activity.[15] Criticism is the major, in its largest sense it is the *only* native American art. Complaints about America's lack of original creativity in the arts miss this point. Responding to, improvising on, 'playing' with, re-creating, synthesizing and interpreting 'given' structures of all kinds, political, social, aesthetic, these have historically constituted the transatlantic mode in our century and before it, to an extent that might now force us to recognize that criticism makes Americans of us all.

My emblem for this will be that critic, for in these terms Fortinbras is one, who enters at the end of *Hamlet* and speaks, in his analysis of it, in the voice of *Telmah*:

> Let four captains
> Bear Hamlet like a soldier to the stage,
> For he was likely, had he been put on,
> To have prov'd most royal; (*pause; then, turning to
> Claudius*) and for *his* passage,
> The soldier's music and the rite of war
> Speak loudly for him.
> Take up the bodies. Such a sight as this
> Becomes the field, but here shows much amiss.
> Go, bid the soldiers shoot.
>
> (V. ii. 400–8)

The equation which that particular inserted intonation permits between the 'mighty opposites', Hamlet and Claudius, effectively turns what we call *Hamlet* momentarily into what I have been terming *Telmah* or, no less effectively, it allows each to be seen at that moment in its most intimate involvement with the other. As the trumpets sound, the moment belongs to Fortinbras, that speculative instrument, in the tonal, or musical, or intonational or dialogic quality of whose utterance these extremes meet. It is not inappropriate, finally – it is not even surprising – that within his name (since this chapter has spoken so much of nomenclature) we should just discern, if we ponder it, the name of the greatest black American jazz trumpeter.

Notes

1 Until recently. See Bert O. States, 'Phenomenology of the curtain call', *Hudson Review*, XXXIV, 3 (Autumn 1981), 371–80.

2 I am guided here by Edmund Leach's excellent account in his *Culture and Communication* (Cambridge, 1976), 74–5.

3 A. J. P. Taylor, *English History 1914–45* (Oxford, 1965), 39.

4 ibid., 40.

5 In 1914, together with R. W. Seton-Watson, Alfred E. Zimmern and Arthur Greenwood, Dover Wilson contributed to a volume called *The War and Democracy* (London, 1914). In a chapter devoted to a comprehensive overview of Russia he wrote of 'the grand simple life they lead in the fields, a life of toil indeed but of toil sweet and infinitely varied', etc. (205). The Russians, he claims, have achieved democracy, have virtually realized all the principles of liberty, fraternity, equality (191), and indeed can be said to have 'discovered the secret of existence' (205).

6 *The Teaching of English in England* (Newbolt Report) (London, HMSO, 1921), 21–2.

7 Cit. Margaret Mathieson, *The Preachers of Culture: A Study of English and its Teachers* (London, 1975), 69–70.

8 *The Teaching of English in England*, 252–3.

9 George Sampson, *English for the English* (Cambridge, 1921, 1925), Preface to 1925 edn, xv. See Mathieson, cit. 74–5.

10 *The Teaching of English in England*, 254.

11 ibid., 255.

12 John Dover Wilson, *What Happens in Hamlet* (Cambridge, 1935), 14.

13 John Dover Wilson, *Milestones on the Dover Road* (London, 1969), 213–14.

14 A valuable exception to this tendency is W. W. Robson's essay, 'Does the king see the dumb-show?', *Cambridge Quarterly*, VI, 4 (1975), 303–26, which reaches similar conclusions, although by a different route. The case for a *Hamlet* of multiple viewpoints, announcing the plurality inherent in the great tragedies, is incisively made.

15 This point has been made and brilliantly developed by Geoffrey Hartman in *Criticism in the Wilderness* (New Haven, 1980).

6

Conclusion: 1917 and All That

English

It was a critical year. In the spring the United States of America declared war on Germany and thus began an involvement in European affairs, as well as in those of the rest of the world, that continues to the present. In the autumn the successful Bolshevik *coup* in Russia completed a revolutionary process and instituted a competing regime that remains in contention both in Europe and beyond.

At various points in the preceding essays it has been suggested that these crucial events of 1917 helped to shape the ways in which influential critics read the plays of Shakespeare: that their readings accordingly reflect, or even represent a covert and unwitting but nevertheless palpable adjustment to the ground-swell of history. It may finally be possible to push the argument a little further than that: to suggest that events rooted in America and Russia significantly helped to generate a context for the study of Shakespeare which lent that activity a distinctive bearing.

The context was formed by the academic subject called 'English'. The entry of America into the war guaranteed, as Sir Walter Raleigh knew, the dominance of English as a world language over its chief competitor, German. The Bolshevik action created, as Dover Wilson and his Newbolt Committee colleagues saw, the need for a bulwark against the spread of revolution. To promote the study of literature written in the

120

world's most powerful language, and at the same time to promote a sense of national cultural coherence that could function internationally as a model of sense and good order seemed an admirable programme. A subject such as 'English' could reasonably hope to fulfil it. There is a tide in the affairs of academe and in 1917 it demanded to be taken at the flood. Thus it was, F. L. Lucas takes up the story, that in March of that year 'while Russia was tottering into revolution and America preparing for war . . . at Cambridge members of the Senate met to debate the formation of an English Tripos'.[1]

Of course, the year 1917 cannot be said to mark the actual birth of the subject: beyond the English pale, in places as otherwise diverse as India and Scotland and even within it at Oxford and in London, syllabuses existed, instruction was under way. But the immense institutional expansion of English, its enormous unprecedented and overwhelming advance in the educational world can certainly be dated from the end of the First World War. The year of the Newbolt Report, 1921, found English irrevocably linked with the notion of a cohesive national culture, identity and purpose, and thus able to be charged by the report, as no academic subject had ever been charged, with the task of conserving and reinforcing that culture, identity and purpose. Its growth proved irresistible. By now, some sort of encounter with English is virtually required by law of the bulk of the population of Britain, North America, Australia, and many another country.

Englishness

Circumstances such as these inevitably foster a complex relationship between the academic subject of English and the culture, identity and purpose which that subject was designed to serve: 'Englishness'. The one sustains, and even helps to create the other. And yet, in the same period since 1917, a series of continuing confrontations has brought just this matter of 'Englishness' into question. Issues raised by events in Ireland and Ulster, the retreat from colonialism followed by immigration from former colonies, the rise of Welsh and Scottish nationalism, the special problems of Africa, membership of the European Economic Community, the Falklands campaign, have all to some degree brought into focus the matter of the definition, limits and specific

121

character of 'Englishness'. And latterly they have done so for millions to whom twenty-five years of cheap travel and television have perhaps also suggested that English culture involves a peculiar and specific way of life, rather than the only or necessarily the most desirable one. It might even be reasonable to detect in the invention of the subject itself a major diagnostic response to an early apprehension of the complexities surrounding cultural identity. Current talk of a 'crisis' in English neglects that history. There is no crisis *in* English. There was and is a crisis which *created* English and of which it remains a distinctive manifestation: a child of Empire's decline, we might say, by America out of Russia.

Making meaning

As that crisis deepens in the latter years of this century, its displaced academic manifestation finds itself pushed more and more into the foreground, as if the problems were in fact located and might even be solved there. A kind of smouldering hysteria has been no stranger to the field of academic literary criticism in Britain for the last fifty years and more. Accusations, denunciations, reports of traitors and double-agents are not unknown. It is almost as if a way of life were under siege.

The latest villain of the piece has seemed to be that most subversive of immigrants to English shores: literary theory. Literary theory not only challenges critical investments and patrimonies, threatening to debase the intellectual currency or people the island with poststructuralists. Worse, it undermines common sense. This, to English eyes, makes it guilty of *lèse-majesté*. For theory argues that all critical analysis, even that (or especially that) which claims to derive from common sense, depends upon and puts into practice a particular framework of presuppositions: that it speaks, not objectively, but from a specific and identifiable standpoint. There can be no criticism which is innocent of theory. There can be no criticism 'itself'. As a result, no innocent, common-sense encounter with any text can be available to us. If we accept it, that argument requires that we examine and make plain the position from which we offer critical judgements. In the present case, it supplies a motive for the attempt to make overt, for instance, the covert positions outlined in some of the preceding essays.

And this itself suggests a larger project: one which would make exactly that process – the construction of cultural meaning and the battle to establish versions of it through the reading of literary texts – the main focus of 'English' itself. We might even, to be outrageous, think of abandoning one of the original, founding notions of the subject: that it should consist of the steadfast, non-theoretical contemplation of self-evidently 'great' works of literary art, undertaken in the belief that this will make us, in some unspecified way, better human beings.

A slight shift of focus brings into view a much more rewarding pursuit. This would involve us in confronting, not the 'great' works of art in themselves – they have in any case no claim to existence 'in themselves' – but the ways in which those works of art have been processed, generated, presented, worked upon, in our own time and previously, as part of the struggle for cultural meaning outlined above. In this form, 'English' would consist, not of a supposedly innocent encounter with literary texts, but of an analysis of the ways in which the meanings of those texts have been produced and used: the study of how readings of them arise, operate, conflict and clash, of the social and political positions which they embody and on behalf of which they function.

This is another way of saying that we should teach our students that texts are texts: that Shakespeare's plays for instance are not transparent entities, giving immediate access to single, coherent, preordained meaning, but inherently plural structures, always open to manifold interpretations. Given our system of broad-based education, they constitute highly significant and sensitive areas in which competing forces within our society struggle for domination. The outcome of that struggle determines a multitude of central priorities and 'realities' of our way of life. In the process, terms such as 'greatness' and 'tradition' and 'authenticity' and 'sincerity' become prizes to be distributed by the victors.

Writing Shakespeare

This book has offered a collection of essays which reflect on some of the ways in which our society processes Shakespeare and awards those prizes, and on some of the purposes for which this is done. The agencies involved include, it has been argued, an education system which by now promotes the subject called 'English' as a major concern and guarantees Shakespeare's centrality within it; the rise of a professional academic criticism with the same end in view; and various economic and social pressures which constitute a formative context.

Of course, the present volume forms part of the same process. There can be no opting out. This is a text: its arguments respond to and are shaped by current economic, social and political pressures, whether overtly or covertly, and they may be read in response to others. Its case has been put by means of specific example for the most part, since this is the preferred mode of most of those whom the essays aim to persuade. Nevertheless, a fundamental theoretical point of view operates throughout, in accordance with the general principle outlined above: that beyond the various readings to which Shakespeare's plays may be subjected, there lies no final, authoritative or essential meaning to which we can ultimately turn. Our 'Shakespeare' is our invention: to read him is to write him.

It follows that the criticism of Shakespeare should be recognized as neither innocent nor transparent, and in line with the shift of focus already mentioned, that it ought to find a place on the syllabus of 'English' itself. The suggestion that the texts of Shakespearian tragedy should finally share the scholar's attention with a text called, say, *Shakespearean Tragedy* may sound perverse. But it emerges readily enough from the simplest questioning of the validity of those inherited polarities, such as writer–reader, or creator–critic, in which our own age has made its curious investment.

Storyville

Jazz music, a quintessential product of our age, certainly questions that deployment. The urgency with which it merges composer and performer, creator and critical analyst, challenges a whole range of analogous polarities as part of the process by which its African mode systematically disconcerts European certainties. For complex historical reasons America has acted as the crucible for this encounter and running throughout the latter part of these essays has been a growing sense of the impingement, in our century, of American concerns on the nature of our experience of Shakespeare's texts. We might recall that 1917 was also the year in which a memorable American voice announced a characteristically tentative and fretful, but none the less obsessive relationship with the Bard:

> No! I am not Prince Hamlet, nor was meant to be;
> Am an attendant lord, one that will do
> To swell a progress, start a scene or two,
> Advise the prince; no doubt, an easy tool,
> Deferential, glad to be of use,
> Politic, cautious, and meticulous;
> Full of high sentence, but a bit obtuse;
> At times, indeed, almost ridiculous –
> Almost, at times, the Fool.[2]

In the circumstances, I have found myself attracted to Geoffrey Hartman's conceit that, as a native American confection, with its unsettling commitment to creative re-presentation and re-interpretation, jazz offers a model for a future notion of literary criticism.[3]

In the present context, that leaves one final point to be made. These essays began with a consideration of aspects of the town of Shakespeare's birth. If jazz music had its Stratford-upon-Avon, it would be located in a place called Storyville, the old red-light district of the city of New Orleans, in the State of Louisiana. According to legend, the music was born and flowered in its brothels and honky-tonks as an accompaniment to their trade, and the New Orleans authorities were careful to confine it within the boundaries of the district. The spread of jazz music to the great northern cities and thence into the popular music of the world at large can be, again according to legend, attributed to the moral concern of the United States Navy Department. Fearful (it claimed) for the welfare of its young sailors, the department mounted and sustained a massive campaign to close Storyville down. It proved successful, despite the fact that the proposals violated or ignored all manner of state and civic rights. The city's administration appealed to the highest level, but to no avail.[4] The New Orleans police force moved in large numbers into the district, the brothels were forcibly closed, the honky-tonks dismantled, the potential rioters rounded up and restrained. Within forty-eight hours an ordinance disestablishing Storyville came into force: jazz music began the long trek north, thence to burst upon an astonished, delighted world. This happened on 10 November 1917, two days after the Bolshevik coup in Russia. It was certainly a critical year.

Notes

1 Cit. Francis Mulhern, *The Moment of Scrutiny* (London, 1979), 3–4.
2 T. S. Eliot, 'The Love Song of J. Alfred Prufrock', in *Prufrock and Other Observations* (London, 1917).
3 See pp. 118–19.
4 Al Rose, *Storyville, New Orleans* (University of Alabama, 1974), 167–8.

Index

Marx, Karl, 38, 107
Mathieson, Margaret, 119
Mensheviks, 108
Mermaid Tavern, 42
Meyer, Kuno, 67
Mill Hill School, 66–7
Miller, Richard, 91
Milton, John, 59
Modern Language Review, 101, 105, 110
Montrose, Louis Adrian, 7, 26
Moorcroft-Wilson, J., 72
Moore, Adam, 8
Moore, G. E., 46
More, Sir Thomas, 9
Morley, John, 56
Mulhern, Francis, 126
Munitions, Ministry of, 104
Murray, Gilbert, 32, 49
Murray, K. M. Elisabeth, 71
music, nature of, 80 ff., 87–90; music and drama, 88–9
music-hall, 90

nationalism, 121
Nature, 1–2, 20 ff., 23–5
New English Dictionary, 55
New Orleans, 125–6
Newbolt, Sir Henry, 111, 112, 115
Newbolt Report, 111–15 *passim*, 120, 121
Nowell-Smith, Simon, 50, 71

Olivier, Sir Laurence, 67
orality, 58, 86
orgasm, 84 ff.
Oxford, 28; Balliol College, 28–30 *passim*, 46, 47; chair of English Literature, 55, 57, 61, 63, 64, 70, 121; Merton chair of English, 30; Professor of Poetry, 30 ff., 47
Oxford English Dictionary, 55

Palmer, D. J., 71
paralanguage, 79–90 *passim*

Parker, Patricia, x
pastoral, 7
Pearson, Hesketh, 49
Petrograd, 104
philosophy, 27, 29, 30, 31
Pirandello, Luigi, 95
Plato, 114
play-text, nature of, 76–90 *passim*
Plutarch, 81–2
popular song, 80–90 *passim*
poststructuralism, 122
Potter, Stephen, ix, 71
puns, 84–5

Quinn, E. G., 90
Quinton, Anthony, 46, 47, 50

ragtime, 85–90 *passim*
Raleigh, Walter Alexander, 57–71 *passim*, 120
Raleigh, Sir Walter, 70–1, 73
Read, Herbert, 91
reading, theory of, 32 ff., 41, 59, 77 ff.
realism, 106
Reform Bill, 1867, 55
Replingham, William, 9
Restoration theatre, 59
Richards, I. A., 91
Richter, Melvin, 29, 49
Ricks, Christopher, 91
Robertson, J. M., 115
Robson, W. W., 119
Rose, Al, 126
Round Table, 108
Royal Air Force, 70
Royal Colonial Institute, 65
Royal Shakespeare Theatre, 1, 13, 24, 25, 26
Ruby, Herman, 81, 90
Russell, Bertrand, 46
Russia, 104–16 ff., 122
Rymer, Thomas, 79

Saint Louis, Missouri, 86
Salisbury, Marquis of, 105
Sampson, George, 119